The Third Book of
Words
to Live By

Selected and Interpreted by
Seventy-eight Eminent Men and Women
Edited by

William Nichols

SIMON AND SCHUSTER

New York   1962

FIRST PRINTING

ACKNOWLEDGMENTS

Permission has been granted to reprint the following material:

"A Thanksgiving Prayer" by Louis Bromfield, reprinted with permission of McGraw-Hill Book Company, Inc., from *Go with God* by Jim Bishop. Copyright © 1958 by Jim Bishop.

"Letter to a Little Girl" by F. Scott Fitzgerald, from *The Crack-Up* by F. Scott Fitzgerald. Copyright 1945 by New Directions. Reprinted by permission of New Directions, Publishers.

"On Meditation" by Dr. R. W. Luxton, from an address published by the *British Medical Journal*, 1957. Reprinted by permission of the magazine and the author.

LIBRARY OF CONGRESS CATALOG CARD NUMBER: 62-9598
MANUFACTURED IN THE UNITED STATES OF AMERICA
BY AMERICAN BOOK–STRATFORD PRESS, INC., NEW YORK

"The way to do is to be"

——LAO-TSE

Contents

PART NINE: WAYS OF LIFE

PART TEN: TALISMANS

PART ELEVEN: LEGACIES

PART TWELVE: FOR A BETTER AMERICA

11

Introduction

THIS IS the third anthology of "Words to Live By" chosen from the pages of *This Week* Magazine. As with the previous collections, it represents a mosaic of what people are thinking and feeling in challenging times.

The "Words to Live By" page has been a regular feature in *This Week* for fifteen years—a fact which is in itself important. It started almost by accident. I have told the story before, but it is worth repeating here, as a reminder of how this series began.

Back in 1947, I came upon a book by David Grayson which told stories of the rural life in his New England village. One described a farmer who, whenever he ran across some bit of prose or verse he liked, slipped the words inside his hatband and later tacked them up on his granary wall.

"I thought afterward," Grayson recalled, *"how most of us have collections of sayings we live by. . . . It would be difficult to find an adult human being who hasn't a saying or*

two, or more, that he is saving because it expresses something vital."

I liked David Grayson's story and reprinted it. Then, more or less as an afterthought, we asked a number of important men and women if they had any sayings they would like to submit.

That started it. Ever since, selections have been arriving in a steady stream, generally with a statement or story to explain why and how the "saying" had become "something vital" in the life of the contributor.

By now, nearly a thousand of these brief articles have appeared in *This Week,* and been read by many among the 14,-000,000 families who regularly receive the magazine each Sunday. The series has turned out to be a unique form of sharing; and, unlike most editorial features, this one simply refuses to grow old or die. On the contrary, there seems to be a process of constant renewal through the rediscovery and restatement of old truths by new people, in terms of new experience.

As part of this process it is perhaps worth noting that the present group of selections, in comparison with previous volumes, shows increasing emphasis on such subjects as honor, duty, integrity, discipline and personal effort and excellence. All of this, I believe, reflects people's current concern with the condition of our country in these days of strain.

As to content, there is one other thing which needs to be said: these little pieces are all frankly "inspirational." This is a word which often causes apprehension, particularly in militantly sophisticated or intellectual circles.

Yet there is also a good deal to be said for inspiration, and I should like to take this occasion to say it. As an editor, I have always believed that to ignore inspiration is to neglect one of the principal functions of communication. This neglect has been a fault with many publications in our time, and may well have been one of the reasons for their decline in favor.

From the beginning, magazines and newspapers have had four major functions—to provide *news, entertainment, instruction,* and *inspiration.* But currently most of them are concentrating on the first three areas, to the almost total exclusion of the last. There was a time when the big national magazines were, above all else, a strong inspirational force throughout the land. That quality is still associated with the names of the "greats" in the national magazines of an earlier era—names like Edward Bok, George Horace Lorimer, John Siddall, Gertrude Lane, Mrs. William Brown Meloney, and many more.

But now, inspiration is in danger of becoming a lost art. The national magazines seem to have lost heart. In the headlong pursuit of readership they have become self-conscious, or cynical, or sophisticated. And in the process I believe they have lost that strong, outflowing force of faith and leadership which once united them so intimately with the American people.

There are only a few other things to say. First, this is not a book to be read at a gallop, or absorbed at one sitting. It is *not* intended for Rapid Readers.

On the contrary, each piece, however brief, represents the expression of some enduring experience in the lifetime of its writer, so it should be read and considered slowly.

Recently Walter J. Couse, a Detroit businessman and *This Week* reader, wrote telling how he uses the previous anthology. His suggestion is such a good one that I should like to pass it along:

> I have developed a habit, and it seems a good habit, of reading one "Words to Live By" excerpt each day. Strangely, I find myself mentally browsing over it many times during the day, and it helps.
>
> My father's boss in Chicago had him take a new word out of the dictionary each day—learn it—learn what it meant—use it in his letters and conversations as often as possible. Dad said at first it was an awful chore, but later a most interesting habit and he enjoyed it. His letters became perfections of English grammar and a pleasure to read. This "Words to Live By" book could have the same end reaction on one's living if followed constantly. I am going to start. I may not finish, but I'll start.

Whether my friend finishes or not, I can forecast the experience which lies before him, since by now I know what happens to thoughtful people when they make a practice of examining the choices and reflections of others. They read them first, simply as bits of wisdom outside their own experience—"touchstones," Matthew Arnold called such pieces. But then they are inevitably caught up in the fascinating game of applying the wisdom of others to their own lives.

Presently they are making their own choices, as David Grayson says, of sayings that contain for them a special and personal truth. Soon they are making their own interpretations, thus converting vague "feelings" into constructive thought.

To show how it works, I have purposely included several cases where two or more pieces have been contributed by the same author—George Mardikian, the genial San Francisco restaurateur; Samuel Goldwyn, the irrepressible Hollywood producer; Howard Van Smith, a Florida newspaperman whose inspired reporting has brought him a Pulitzer Prize. And, as you will see on pages 36 and 215, I have tried it myself. Editors are supposed to be notoriously reluctant writers, but even so, I can commend this form of writing. It is an interesting and agreeable exercise in self-understanding.

And now, it is only natural to end this Introduction with a selection. The one I have chosen is from the writings of that splendid American, Ralph Waldo Emerson, who has inspired so many of the contributions to this book. In one of

17

his most enduring sayings, he takes the ancient Biblical words, and adds to them, as follows:

> "Man does not live by bread alone,
> but by *faith*, by *admiration* and
> by *sympathy*."

It is my greatest hope that, in the shared experiences on the following pages, you will discover something of all three.

—WILLIAM NICHOLS

New York
Autumn 1961

PART ONE

On Growing Up

"LIVE YOUR LIFE while you have it. Life is a splendid gift. There is nothing small in it. For the greatest things grow by God's Law out of the smallest. But to live your life you must discipline it. You must not fritter it away in 'fair purpose, erring act, inconstant will' but make your thoughts, your acts all work to the same end and that end, not self but God. That is what we call character."

—FLORENCE NIGHTINGALE

LOVE TO AUNT LIZ by Edward Weeks
THE HAPPIEST MAN by David Niven
ON QUESTIONS by Bergen Evans
ON HARD KNOCKS—I by James Cagney
ON HARD KNOCKS—II by April Oursler Armstrong
THE HIDDEN POWER by Lewis L. Strauss
BRIGHT BEGINNINGS by Justice Thomas C. Clark
ON BEING RIGHT by William Nichols
WHY EVERYTHING COUNTS by Samuel Goldwyn

Love to Aunt Liz

BY

EDWARD WEEKS

AUTHOR, LECTURER, AND EDITOR OF
''THE ATLANTIC MONTHLY''

"Keep going!"

—MY AUNT LIZ

A BOY would be lucky to have a godmother like my Aunt Liz. She was the oldest of my mother's five sisters, and she helped bring them up when Grandma became an invalid. She had her beaux, but she never married, her nephews became her family and what she gave each of us was unforgettable. To us her looks never changed: she was spare and tall with her gray hair drawn back into a bun; her eyes were what held you.

After Grandma's death, she kept house for my grandfather, the Colonel, and here dwelt loyalty. As a girl she had shaken hands with Mr. Lincoln and had visited Meade in his headquarters and, unforced, she passed on to us her love for the flag. When I came down with whooping cough, I was shipped off to Aunt Liz to keep me away from the kids, and during my quarantine she proposed that we read the Bible together, which we did at bedtime and omitting the "begats." The readings were continued for years after, whenever we were together.

I was a runt and no good at athletics, but Aunt Liz was sure that I could excel in English and kept finding things for me to memorize and recite—not the old chestnuts, but a short story like "Wee Willie Winkie," by Kipling, or "Fables in Slang," by George Ade.

She did things with us for fun, like collecting moonstones on the beach before breakfast; she remembered my fondness for butterscotch kisses; she was someone you could talk to about girls. In answer to one of my misspelled effusions she wrote, "You misspelled 'together'; think of it as 'to-get-her' and you won't do so again." And when I was courting in earnest and had told her I hoped to be engaged, she wrote: "Grandmother Halsey used to say marriage was two wild animals—Bear and Forebear"—quaint words whose truth I appreciated later.

When at last she was on her own in that boardinghouse room, papered with family photographs, she became a librarian; she had a gift for helping others to find the right books. She talked of writing a simplified speller, and on my birthday she still sent me a box of pencils, as if to say "Keep going." How can you thank a person as selfless as that, a maiden aunt, for bringing out the self-confidence, the loyalty, the resourcefulness you never knew you possessed? Not by words. By being.

The Happiest Man

BY

DAVID NIVEN

MOTION PICTURE ACTOR

"It all balances."

—FRANK GOODALL

THE HAPPIEST MAN I've ever known was a fisherman named Frank Goodall on the Isle of Wight, off the southern coast of England. He never set foot in our house there, but he had more to do with bringing me up than anyone—a sort of substitute father.

My father had been killed at the Dardanelles in 1915, and Mother was left with four of us. She was French, splendid, and very vague. Now suddenly we were augmented by a disastrous stepfather. He took a pretty dim view of all of us,

24

but he detested me and I was packed off to boarding school at six.

Those were the days of the great bullies in English public schools, the days, too, of shell-shocked masters with a sad, sadistic streak. When, at the age of seven, I couldn't master a Latin conjugation, I was stuck out of a fourth-floor class-room window and the window closed down on my back while I was soundly thrashed.

But summers and Easter vacation I went home to the Isle of Wight and told old Frank, the fisherman, all about it. Many as my problems were, with his help I managed to laugh them off. He taught me to fish, to catch lobster by hand, all the love of nature that has stood me in good stead ever since.

But above all, he gave me a piece of advice that has come to bear time and again on my adult life. He said, "I've been fishing for fifty years. You have a run of luck, then some days you'll have nothing, not even a nibble. It all balances." He couldn't have given me more needed wisdom.

I've remembered his words many times when things were grim and also when they were going especially well—for it's just as important not to lose your head with joy either, especially in a business where the graph of your career resembles a roller coaster. Through all my ups and downs, I have thought of old Frank Goodall and remembered that the happiest man I ever knew was a man for whom sometimes the fish were biting and sometimes not.

On Questions

BY

BERGEN EVANS

TEACHER AND TV QUIZ EXPERT

"He that nothing questioneth, nothing learneth."

—THOMAS FULLER

I THINK one of the most fruitful moments in my life came when my old zoology professor, Dr. Stephen Williams of Miami University, in Ohio, whom I greatly respected, told me that he would give any student an A in his course who asked one intelligent question.

Up to that time I had assumed that intelligence consisted of giving answers. Now I began to see that the question is as much a part of knowledge as the answer—often the more important part. Because it's the question that shows us what we don't know.

Men had assumed from the beginning of time that a heavier object fell faster than a lighter one—until Galileo said, "Does it?" Men had marveled at the giraffe's neck for thousands of years before Darwin asked, "Why?"

But it isn't just scientists who should ask questions. No one knows all the answers and if he thinks he does he has stopped thinking and growing. Part of being alive and in touch with the world around and within you lies in searching for your own answers, in asking your own questions.

It has been 36 years since my old teacher startled me with his pronouncement. For 30 of those years I have myself been a teacher. Most of the facts he taught me—most of the answers he gave me—have long been forgotten. But I have not forgotten that a questioning student is more important than an answering teacher.

On Hard Knocks—I

BY
JAMES CAGNEY

MOVIE STAR

"The biggest problem in the world could have been solved when it was small."

—WITTER BYNNER

I'VE HAD my share of problems, as who hasn't? I learned when I was young to try to face them, and to work them out before they got too big.

My father, a saloonkeeper in New York City, died in the flu epidemic after World War I. There were four of us Cagney brothers from 19 down to 14 years old, and soon after his death, our baby sister Jeanne came along. We had no money. We four boys went to work, supported ourselves and our mother and sister, and kept going to school, too. Two of my brothers worked their way through medical school, and they're successful doctors today.

I remember one year I got home from school at two in the afternoon. I'd do my homework and take a nap before going to work as a bellhop at the Friars' Club. I worked until three in the morning, and I had to be back in school at eight.

During one vacation, I wrapped bundles for Wanamaker's department store during the day. At night I was a switchboard operator and attendant (and sort of general bouncer) at a pool hall. On Sunday, my day off, I sold tickets for the Hudson River Day Line.

It was good for me. I feel sorry for the kid who has too cushy a time of it. Ultimately he has to come face to face with the realities of life without any papa or mama to do his thinking for him.

Of course, it's natural for parents to want to protect their youngsters. But this can be overdone. Sooner or later, life gives everybody troubles—no one gets away with smooth sailing all the way.

I think that if you learn how to take the knocks when you're young, you're a lot better able to handle them later on. I'm not saying that because I had it tough when I was a kid, I don't make mistakes. I've made lots of them and still do. But the kind of training I had taught me to face my problems head on—and as soon as possible.

❀❀❀

On Hard Knocks — II

BY
APRIL OURSLER ARMSTRONG

WRITER AND MOTHER

"You can see farther in the dark than in the day."

—UNKNOWN

AS A CHILD I was told that every cloud had a silver lining, that nothing happened without a reason, and that what seemed to be tragedy was, actually, a blessing in disguise. This was hard for my young mind to understand. As I grew older it became still harder to understand, even though experience had given me my own practical proof of it.

I remember my father, Fulton Oursler, sitting in his great library window with a storm-troubled bay framed behind him. I've forgotten now the cause of my 11-year-old grief, but it was to me severe sorrow. My father said: "April, God sends the darkness of trouble not to punish us, but as a gift —even if we don't know why He gave it to us."

It was a time of darkness for him then, though I, in my ignorance, did not know it. Out of that darkness came his inspirational book on the life of Jesus, *The Greatest Story Ever Told*.

As I grew older I learned for myself that darkness does indeed bring one closer to God. The illnesses of my own children, financial worries, loneliness, the death without warning of my parents, each of these things was a lesson in faith and love.

But why? Why should God choose trouble as the path to Him?

I found my answer in a book now lost, in a sentence I have come to live by. At first reading it seemed nonsense:

"Remember—you can see farther in the dark than in the day!"

I read it again, and suddenly understood.

In the dazzling light of day we cannot see beyond our own world. The sun that delights us keeps our eyes earthbound. But the night gently forces us to lift our eyes to the stars.

You cannot see the stars in daylight. Nor can you see God so clearly in the noontime of happiness.

It's not enough just to know in the daytime that the stars are still there. We know—but we forget them. If He did not send the night, we would not see the stars.

If He did not send darkness to our lives, we might not ever see that we need Him—for light, for love, for joy.

The secret is to open your eyes . . . to see in darkness as in light.

The Hidden Power

BY

LEWIS L. STRAUSS

FORMER CHAIRMAN, ATOMIC ENERGY
COMMISSION, AUTHOR OF "MEN
AND DECISIONS"

"As he thinketh in his heart, so is he."

—PROVERBS 23:7

IT IS SO MUCH easier to control our actions than our thoughts. Law and public sanctions help us keep our deeds in line—but only Conscience polices our thoughts.

Not long ago, meeting with several aging classmates, we talked about the events that had left their marks upon us when we were in high school together. Above all else, one occasion stood out clearly in all our minds. It was the day, nearly 50 years ago, when the governor of a distant state spoke at our high school assembly in my home town in Virginia. His theme was that a boy could mold his future as a man by the kind of thoughts he encouraged, and those he forbade himself to think. The text he used was, "As a man thinketh in his heart, so is he."

That thought, of all those brought to us as youngsters, made so deep an impression upon our minds that not one of us had forgotten it.

❀❀❀

Bright Beginnings

BY
THOMAS C. CLARK

ASSOCIATE JUSTICE,
UNITED STATES SUPREME COURT

❀

"Of a good beginning cometh a good end."

—JOHN HEYWOOD

BACK IN 1912 (only two years after the organization was founded), I joined the Boy Scouts of America and became an Eagle Scout in 1914. My troop, No. 1 in Dallas, was a drum and bugle corps. There being no other marching units available at that time, our troop was designated by the city fathers to lead all parades.

Some say my interest in this activity stemmed from the ensuing half-day school holidays. However that may be, the experience struck the spark that led to my ambition to follow a public career. It has carried me from my days as a lawyer to civil district attorney, then Attorney General of the United States, and finally to the United States Supreme Court.

Of course, it takes a lot more than the fun of leading a parade to make a man a good public servant or a good citizen. And the many clubs, groups, organizations and agencies, like the Boy Scouts, which deal with youth supply a lot more than parades and fun.

But of all the things they supply, the most important, I believe, are sparks. By exposing youngsters to healthy kinds of living and doing and working, and to people they can admire and emulate, the organized youth groups strike sparks of ambition and interest, character and pride that light fires for a lifetime. They are the kind of fires which cast their light and warmth throughout the community.

On Being Right

BY

WILLIAM NICHOLS

EDITOR OF ''THIS WEEK'' MAGAZINE

"There's a Harvard man on the wrong side of every question."

—A. LAWRENCE LOWELL

WHEN I WAS a boy I used to think that somewhere out ahead lay a magic moment when one would be grown up, and know all the answers. At that point life would be easy: no more doubts, no more uncertainties. In any given situation, one would always know exactly what to do.

Since then, many years have gone by, and the only thing I have really learned is that the moment of absolute certainty never comes. Along the way, while looking for the answers, I had the treat of knowing the late president of

36

Rec'd by CL
Jan 24 65

Harvard, A. Lawrence Lowell. Some of his salty sayings were better than a college degree.

Once, for example, he said: "There's a Harvard man on the wrong side of every question." It was his way of making the point that each of us is different and that no one can ever know all the answers all the time.

Another of his favorite sayings went this way: "The mark of an educated man is the ability to make a reasoned guess on the basis of insufficient information."

What can we infer from Lowell's observations? Simply this: that often, when a man is faced with a decision, it is impossible for him to fill in all the uncertainties. He cannot be *sure* he has every fact. And so, in deciding, he must guess. But this is precisely the point at which "education" comes in. For true education goes far beyond facts. It means more than classrooms and lectures and examinations. Education also means *experience* and *faith, courage* and *understanding*. Most of all it means *the ability to think and act*. These are the qualities which translate dead knowledge into living wisdom. They are what make our "guesses" turn out right.

Why Everything Counts

BY

SAMUEL GOLDWYN

FAMOUS HOLLYWOOD PRODUCER

"You always meet people a second time."

—UNKNOWN

THOSE WORDS were told to me when I was quite young, and whether I have fully succeeded or not, I have at least always tried to act accordingly. I know of no better advice to pass on—especially to young people.

The first impressions you make are usually the most important. What you say—what you do—how you act—the first time you meet someone, will largely determine your reception the next time. Even though it may be years later, people will usually remember whether you were courteous or rude, decent or smart-alecky, honest or dishonest, and the general impression you made.

Be yourself with everyone you meet—but be your best self, for you can be sure that before you have lived out your life, you are going to meet again.

 PART TWO

On Doing
and Being

"Man is effective in the world not only through what he does, but above all through what he is."
—RUDOLF STEINER

On Seeing Clearly

BY

EMILY KIMBROUGH

NOTED TRAVELER, LECTURER, WRITER

"Nonsense! That would never be noticed from a trotting horse."

—MY GRANDMOTHER

A FEW WEEKS ago, as I was mounting the steps to a lecture platform, my stocking caught on a sharp edge and was very nearly disintegrated by a run. I paused dismayed, but at that instant's pause a phrase of my grandmother's came back to me.

When a small thing upset someone my grandmother used to say, "Nonsense! That would never be noticed from a trotting horse."

This pronouncement was first directed at me when I was ten. I was complaining bitterly of some defect in my appearance which I thought was bound to draw the attention of every guest at the party for which I was being made ready. Grandmother's image of a trotting horse was impressive to a little girl. I had to admit that a horseman riding by would not notice my shortcoming.

I think I began then to sort out the things that are important from the unimportant.

Through the years, I have conjured up often that ghostly rider. He has become for me an unfailing authority for my own scale of values—important vs. trivial. Have I said or done something unkind, or was it only harmlessly awkward? Have I evaded those things that I ought to have done, or were they not worth doing in the first place? Conversely, have I bridled at an evidence of malice on someone else's part, or was I making something of nothing at all?

In my mind I sometimes cause the rider of the trotting horse to dismount and allow me to take his place. I have found that the back of a trotting horse is also a good site from which to set in proper scale one's personal landscape. It is surprising how many petty annoyances disappear entirely when one rides by them on a trotting horse.

On Walking Freely

BY

DR. EDWIN ROBERTS

MINISTER

"Happiness is a homemade article."

—PROVERB

A FRIEND once said to Ralph Waldo Emerson, "The world is coming to an end tonight," to which Emerson replied, "I can get along without it."

I read this statement once again recently, and it impressed me as one of the wisest ways to approach life that I had ever found. People who live by this philosophy are able to have real happiness.

The secret that Emerson uncovered was that the only way to be able to enjoy anything on this earth is to be willing to part with it. Without this approach to life, anxiety stands between us and the enjoyment of everything.

43

If we cling to our possessions too tightly, our worry for their well-being keeps us from full enjoyment. If we feel that we could not exist without our youth, we will be old before we have found the good life. If we believe we could not stand to live without good health, each minor ache or pain fills us with apprehension. We can secure full enjoyment from the applause of people, only if we know that we can be happy when no one is cheering us. Most important, with the people we love, we must be able to say to ourselves that we could and would go on even if we should have to part with them.

Money had always seemed to me to be the prime essential for foreign travel. But once in the city of Naples I was robbed of my money and thought I could not go on in a country where I did not speak the language and where I had no friends. Then I remembered that I was still strong and had a thumb I could use on the highway.

That trip up Italy was just about the happiest of my life. People gave me rides, fed me, restored my faith in the goodness of life, and brought me to Florence and a bank draft from the United States.

But once again I learned that the way to enjoy anything in life is to know that you can get along without it.

On Speaking Fairly

BY

WILLIAM BRANDON

NOVELIST AND SHORT STORY WRITER

"An old man said, 'See that thou despise not the brother that stands by thee: for thou knowest not whether the spirit of God be in thee or in him.'"

—MARTIN, ABBOT OF DUMES

THESE ARE words I only read recently. They're from a book called *The Desert Fathers,* translations from the Latin by the brilliant Helen Waddell, whose translations from anything should be read by everybody instantly. This particular saying is ascribed to Martin, Abbot of Dumes, a hermit of 1400 years ago.

But I'm beginning to live by it, at least somewhat. I'm being forced. The saying has already become part of our pri-

45

vate family language, and it seems the rest of the family uses it most often on me.

Incredibly reasonable though I know I am at all times, I am occasionally accused of being just a shade too positive I'm right. And then my wife says sweetly, "Thou knowest not . . ."

And it gives me pause. It's a great line and a great thought. It's particularly applicable to the sanctimonious, the holier-than-thou's. (Naturally not me, or even you; I mean those other types.) It's particularly applicable to our cocksure scientific age, our cocksure nation, lolling on the top of the heap and admiring itself in a mirror. (Perhaps some of the recent jolts we've had will help us learn its truth.)

How many of the world's ills stem from the absolute conviction on someone's part that he's right? This is humanity's most dangerous disease—it produces the Torquemadas and Hitlers and the indignant gentleman who deliberately runs into you because he is sure he has the right of way.

These words are words that call for the remedy Socrates used to master his own soul—a little unsureness.

It's a medicine that can be good for individuals and for nations and even for the age in which they live. For thou knowest not . . .

On Reading

BY

CLIFTON FADIMAN

WRITER AND LECTURER

*"He that loves reading has everything within his
reach."*

—WILLIAM GODWIN

MOST OF US have a Lifetime Savings Plan. We don't like
to go along life's road with nothing in our pockets. But how
about going along it with nothing in our minds?

The man I pity most is the one who experiences this
wonderful world, and leaves it without ever quite knowing
what his life has been about. Whatever the state of his bank
account, he lives and dies mentally bankrupt.

So set yourself a Lifetime Reading Plan! Such a grand de-
sign can fill your mind, slowly, gradually, year by year over

the whole of your life, with what the greatest writers of our Western civilization have thought and felt.

The contemporary man who has shared these thoughts and feelings will understand how he has emerged out of 3000 years of history. He will know how he got the ideas by which he lives. He will feel buoyed up by the great and noble stream of Western civilization of which he is a part.

Books are only one key to these discoveries. But the wisest men agree that they are probably the best key. Enjoy them. There's nothing solemn about feeling your mind stretch. It's the most rewarding feeling in the world. These books are an adventure. Reading is not a passive experience—unless you're reading trash. It can be one of the most vigorous forms of living. A good book, like healthy exercise, can give you that pleasant sense of fatigue which comes of having stretched your mental muscles.

On Courage—I

BY

ALFRED LANSING

AUTHOR OF
"ENDURANCE: SHACKLETON'S
INCREDIBLE VOYAGE"

"Men wanted for Hazardous Journey. Small wages, bitter cold, long months of complete darkness, constant danger, safe return doubtful. Honor and recognition in case of success."

—SIR ERNEST SHACKLETON

SIR ERNEST SHACKLETON was an Antarctic explorer. To recruit men for one of his expeditions, he ran the forthright want ad quoted above in a London newspaper.

Sir Ernest wasn't joking. The ad proved grimly prophetic for the brave men who volunteered for the three Antarctic expeditions he led. On one, the ship itself was lost, along with most of the supplies. The men spent 21 months in a living nightmare, camped on drifting ice or struggling toward civilization in three tiny boats.

Yet the men who had signed up for the "hazardous journey" not only refused to give up—they somehow managed to remain cheerful. And they won. Every last one of them returned to civilization alive.

In his want ad, Shackleton had promised "honor and recognition"— and it was heaped upon them. But actually they had earned something much, much greater. Shackleton himself later sought to put it into words: "We pierced the veneer of outside things," he wrote. "We suffered, starved and triumphed, groveled down yet grasped at glory . . . we reached the naked soul of man."

Nowadays, it seems, security is all-important. Too often, I feel, we are satisfied to play it safe, to aim only for the "sure thing." And while most of us still dream of making some sort of "hazardous journey" in our lives, not very many really make them. As a result, our lives may be safer and saner—but we may in the end be making a world in which fewer and fewer ever catch a glimpse of the magnificent naked soul of man.

On Courage—II

BY

CARLO LEVI

AUTHOR OF
"CHRIST STOPPED AT EBOLI"

"Rejoiceth as a strong man to run a race."

—PSALMS 19:5

TRUE COURAGE smiles. It cannot express itself otherwise. Courage is the prime virtue, the necessary element of existence, the birth of everything. Because it is in itself all positive, and cannot be divorced from love and creation, it is in itself happy—the only happiness—and a smile is the only form it can take on the human face.

The archaic smile of the ancient gods and heroes identified them. In less mythological times, such as ours, the same smile returns on the humble features of millions of unknown

51

men and women, when they find in themselves the basic form of courage: the courage of living.

We have all met many great heroes, men who consciously lived and died for freedom. But the infinite mass of obscure men, who daily accept reality with a smile, manifest a silent courage that makes life worthy of being lived.

On Decisiveness

BY

WILLIAM G. SALTONSTALL

PRINCIPAL OF THE
PHILLIPS EXETER ACADEMY

"Begin, be bold, and venture to be wise."

—HORACE

ONE OF our human failings, as I see it, has been our admiration for the "middle-of-the-roader." Certainly many of us agree that the exercise of restraint is one of the marks of the good man. But in some areas compromise is flabby and dangerous. Any person of real conviction and strength must choose one side of the road or the other. It would be a strange kind of education that urged us to be "relatively" honest, "sometimes" just, "usually" tolerant, "for the most part" decent.

As you read history and biography, I think you will not come to equate greatness with compromise. Rather, you will find it in decisiveness, combined with charity, gentleness and justice. There will be some wrong decisions, of course, but as long as mistakes are recognized, the loss is far less serious than that occasioned by playing the middle of the road, sitting on the fence, undecided, unconvinced, incapable of strong feeling.

Life should be a continuing search for those people, those ideas and those causes to which we can gladly and wholly give ourselves.

On Integrity

BY

SAMUEL GOLDWYN

FAMOUS HOLLYWOOD PRODUCER

"To thine own self be true."

—WILLIAM SHAKESPEARE

IT IS hardly a secret that I never attended Harvard or Oxford. The only formal education I ever had was what little I was able to acquire at the night school I attended while working in a factory during the days. Although I do not pretend to be a Shakespearean scholar, I have always considered his words above as one of the soundest possible guides to successful living. And when I say successful I mean it in every sense of the word.

In all the years I have been in Hollywood, I have had one basic advice for the actors or actresses who were trying

55

to be like the current film favorite, for the directors trying to copy someone else's style, for the writers trying to imitate more successful authors, for everyone trying to be something other than what he really was—"Be yourself."

For that is my own way of saying "To thine own self be true"—and it is only by being oneself that an artist can keep his artistic integrity or any human being can preserve his personal integrity.

Being true to yourself—having integrity—means more than just not pretending to be someone else. It means being completely true to what is inside you—to what you know is right. It means doing what you feel you must do, regardless of the immediate cost or sacrifice. It means making decisions for yourself and your family and your entire life, based on what is proper, not on what is expedient. It means at all times to be honorable and to behave decently. And in a very practical sense it pays, for without integrity no person is complete, and without it no book, no play, nothing written, nothing done by man has any real value.

On Honor

BY

GENERAL MARK W. CLARK

PRESIDENT OF THE CITADEL,
MILITARY COLLEGE OF SOUTH CAROLINA

"A Cadet does not lie, or cheat, or steal."

—THE CITADEL HONOR CODE

I HAVE always believed that everyone needs to impose upon himself some rigid code of personal ethics. The Ten Commandments are probably the most perfect example of such a code.

But it seems to me that young people, who perhaps need rules of conduct the most, tend to shy away from long or complex lists of "do's" and "don'ts." That is why we at The Citadel have established our Honor Code which consists of just one rule expressed in nine words: "A Cadet does not lie, or cheat, or steal."

Just nine words. But what important words they are, for without them none can hope to build a decent or a happy life.

Of course, The Citadel's Honor Code is only a beginning. Of course, our 2,000 Cadets know that there is more to character than merely not lying, cheating or stealing. But these negatives are important as a starting point. A man can then go on from these "don'ts" to more positive rules of life. If, as a boy, he learns what not to do, then as he matures, the positive values will slowly move into place. "Do unto others . . ." "Love thy neighbor . . ."—these "do's" are the true capstones of a moral code. But the "don'ts," learned in childhood, are its foundation.

On Self-Respect

BY

PHYLLIS McGINLEY

PULITZER PRIZE POET,
AUTHOR OF "TIMES THREE"

"Don't let your sins turn into bad habits."

—ST. TERESA OF AVILA

THE WOMAN I quote was one of the wittiest, holiest, most delightful creatures who ever lived. She was speaking to a nun of her order, an overscrupulous girl who came to her in tears, berating her own evil nature. "Ah, my dear," Teresa consoled her, "all of us are human and prone to sin. Just see to it that you don't let your sins turn into bad habits."

The paradox is as full of common sense as it is of the saint's famous salty humor. Certainly to err is human, and

Teresa knew it as well as the poet Alexander Pope. It is not the occasional lapse but the repeated fault which turns us into the sort of persons we do not wish to be. We can all mourn a trouble. It's the habit of self-pity which corrodes character. To fly into a rage now and then is excusable. But to let a habit of anger master us is to court destruction. We all like gossip, it's the amusing small change of conversation. But a habit of malice can turn us into bores, troublemakers, monsters of mischief.

Few of us are murderers or traitors or thieves. Yet unkindness is a sin, too, and so is selfishness or intemperance or spite or hate or sloth or detraction. And how many of us are altogether free of those flaws? Wisdom lies in the ability to forgive ourselves such human failings—to tumble, pick ourselves up, shake the dust off our spirits, and try to avoid the next mistake.

No matter what degree of religious faith we profess, all of us yearn to be decent people and we believe in free will. Teresa has given us the best possible advice to follow on the thorny, difficult road to self-respect.

On Hope

BY

THE REVEREND
JOHN LAFARGE, S.J.

FAMOUS CATHOLIC EDITOR AND AUTHOR

"Hope does not disappoint."

—ST. PAUL

I HAVE LEARNED that you can build a life upon hope, and if that principle is your anchor, plenty of other people will cast their moorings hard by you.

Life has taught me that the hopeful policy wins acceptance from even embittered minds. The prophet of despair gains a shouting audience. But one who speaks from hope will be heard long after the noise dies down.

As St. Paul said, "Hope does not disappoint." It is man's answer to the trust placed in him by the Creator.

PART THREE

On Loving
and Liking

"Love is something eternal—the aspect may change, but not the essence. There is the same difference in a person before and after he is in love as there is in an unlighted lamp and one that is burning. The lamp was there and it was a good lamp, but now it is shedding light, too, and that is its real function."

—VINCENT VAN GOGH

WHAT IS LOVE? by Erich Fromm

A WORLD TO LOVE by Ethel Barrymore

ELIXIR OF LOVE by Ilka Chase

I LOVE LIFE by Willie Snow Ethridge

ON LIKING YOURSELF by Robert Paul Smith

"BUT I LIKE YOU" by Myles Connolly

LET'S BREAK BREAD by George D. Mardikian

TO BE A FRIEND . . . by Robert Hardy Andrews

What is Love?

BY

ERICH FROMM

AUTHOR OF "THE ART OF LOVING"

"There is only one kind of love, but it has a thousand guises."

—LA ROCHEFOUCAULD

THE DEEPEST NEED of man is the need to overcome his separateness, to leave the prison of his aloneness. The full answer to the problem of existence lies in true and mature love.

What is mature love? It is union under the condition of preserving one's integrity, one's individuality. Love is an active power, a power which breaks through the walls which separate man from his fellow man. Love overcomes the sense of isolation and separateness, yet it permits you to be yourself. In love the paradox occurs that two beings become one and yet remain two.

A World to Love

BY

ETHEL BARRYMORE

BELOVED ACTRESS OF STAGE AND SCREEN

*"Oh, earth, you're too wonderful for anybody to real-
ize you. Do any human beings ever realize life while
they live it?—every, every minute?"*

—THORNTON WILDER, Emily, in *Our Town*

YOU MUST LEARN day by day, year by year, to broaden
your horizon. The more things you love, the more you are
interested in, the more you enjoy, the more you are indignant
about—the more you have left when anything happens.

I suppose the greatest thing in the world is loving people
and wanting to destroy the sin but not the sinner. And not
to forget that when life knocks you to your knees—well,
that's the best position in which to pray, isn't it? On your
knees. That's where I learned.

66

EDITOR'S NOTE: *Ethel Barrymore, who died in 1959 at the age of 79, brought more than a commanding presence and faultless technique to her long, distinguished theatrical career. She was a woman of rare insight and understanding, as this expression of her personal philosophy so eloquently reveals.*

Elixir of Love

BY

ILKA CHASE

WRITER, ACTRESS, TV STAR

"Love is the salt of life."

—JOHN SHEFFIELD

A LADY I once knew was given a recipe by an old Spanish friend. It told how many cups of this and how many spoonfuls of that were to be used and the length of cooking time, and then her friend added, "However, my dear Clarita, if you want the recipe to be truly a success, you must add grace."

Add grace—which is just another way of saying, add love.

This applies to everything we undertake. To act with honor, intelligence and common sense is admirable, but to know the true sweetness of living we must add grace.

There never was a time when the world was so filled with

neat recipes. We are told exactly how to do everything—from cooking a goose to getting along with our husbands. And many of these instructions will work, too. But unless you bring love into them, unless you add grace, the true flavor of life will be lacking.

Whatever recipe you follow, don't leave out the best ingredient of all. Whatever you do, add grace.

I Love Life

BY
WILLIE SNOW ETHRIDGE

LECTURER AND AUTHOR
OF "RUSSIAN DUET"

*"Nothing great was ever achieved without enthusi-
asm."*

—RALPH WALDO EMERSON

A YEAR or so after I married my husband, Mark, we moved
to New York where an old and dear friend of his, Mike
Witman, then lived. Immediately Mark took me to meet
him and spend a quiet evening talking. It was in that blessed
interim between wars—World War I and II—and the conversation was mostly small talk.

First, the subject of movies came up, and I in my youthful, carried-away manner cried, "I adore the movies."

Then baseball came up and I cried, "I adore baseball."

Then gardening and I cried, "I adore gardening."

Then dancing and I cried, "I adore dancing."

Then fishing and I—yes, I did—I cried, "I adore fishing."

And then this so-called friend of Mark's cried, "Oh, hush. You adore too damned much!"

Naturally I didn't adore this, but it made a deep impression on me. Maybe I wasn't discriminating enough. Maybe in enjoying so much, I was too frivolous and naïve. Maybe it would be smart of me to put a tight curb on my likes.

So, for a while I wouldn't try new things for fear if I tried them I'd love them. I wouldn't go to see a hockey game, a tennis tournament, a prize fight, a polo match. I wouldn't try skiing, tap dancing, bridge, mah-jongg (rook was my game). I wouldn't touch a cigarette.

Then I began to write what I call informal-essay-autobiographical books about my everyday living in the South, and it dawned on me that my one ace in the hole was my enthusiasm for so many things, especially so many little, seemingly insignificant, run-of-the-mine things.

The big events are too few and far between and, frequently, when they do come are disappointing. What makes life full, rich and worth while are the small happenings: gathering pecans with the children on a brisk fall afternoon; setting out tomato plants in the moist spring; riding the bus to town with a gossipy driver; showing friends the pale pink peonies and deep blue iris blooming simultaneously as they should. . . .

This lesson was important to me as a writer, but more than that, it also became deeply significant to me as a person.

On Liking Yourself

BY

ROBERT PAUL SMITH

AUTHOR OF ''WHERE DID YOU GO? OUT,
WHAT DID YOU DO? NOTHING''

*"If we could learn to like ourselves, even a little,
maybe our cruelties and angers might melt away."*

—JOHN STEINBECK

CONSIDERING that I can rarely find anything in my files, it seems wholly right and proper that I do not know the name of the man who said to me: "Don't get hostile with yourself."

But I do remember that he was a Negro jazz musician and it was in a South Side Chicago joint very late one night, back in the 'thirties.

At that time I was very busy being a success: I had a

job with a jazz band, I made $125 a week, I had $100 a week expense money, credit cards for airlines and hotels.

I was 21 years old, and I was wholly miserable. My job was good, but what I wanted more than anything else was to be writing what later became my first novel.

All the sage ones kept telling me my job was a golden opportunity, and since the sage ones were older, I kept on working. But the conflict played havoc with my peace of mind. I was attempting to drink all the booze in the bars. And living without sleep. And trying to travel faster than the speed of light.

This night I had been sitting in a South Side joint telling a musician what a wonderful musician he was, what a terrible musician his opposite number in the band was, what a monster the bandleader was, and eventually what a craven louse I was myself.

He sipped his drink, looked at me benignly, and said in his solemn voice, "Don't get hostile with yourself."

At the time I didn't know what the words meant, but I had an idea there must be something behind them so I remembered them until I did know what they meant. They mean that the one person in the world with whom you have to live continually, closely, and irrevocably is yourself.

You are your own unsleeping judge and jury and jailer, you sit in judgment on yourself, you fix and execute sentence, and you very rarely will listen to appeals in your own behalf.

It does not matter (assuming you are within the law)

whether other people think what you are doing is right. It does not even matter whether they think it is entertaining, useful, or lucrative, or if they wish they could do what you do, or live the way you do.

What matters is whether it seems proper to you, what matters is what verdict you bring in on yourself: friendly, or hostile. In short, do you really like yourself?

"But I Like You"

BY

MYLES CONNOLLY

AUTHOR OF
"THE BUMP ON BRANNIGAN'S HEAD"

"Lord, make me an Instrument of Thy Peace. Where there is hatred, let me sow love. Where there is injury, pardon. . . ."

—ST. FRANCIS OF ASSISI

THE GAME of Cowboys and Indians had been going on vigorously and, to stretch the meaning of the word a little, peacefully, out on the beach for some time. Then, suddenly, there was trouble.

One of the youngsters, a brown-haired Cowboy, about seven and the youngest of the lot, had been captured by the Indians and was to be tied to a stake—the stake being a huge, ugly hunk of driftwood that looked very much like the gnarled roots of an ancient tree. The brown-haired Cowboy objected to being tied to the driftwood. Whether, in his concept of the game, the driftwood was not legitimately a stake or whether he, out of some special sensitivity, found the ugly driftwood objectionable, I could not make out. But he was very definite about it. He would not be tied to it.

The boss of the game, the oldest of the boys, about ten or eleven and something of a bully, grew angry.

"Go on home, Yellow!" he shouted at the little fellow. "Go on home. We don't like you!"

The other boys, in the natural spirit of the gang, took up the words in a sort of singsong. "Go on home, Yellow! We don't like you!"

The boy, hurt and bewildered by this sudden show of cruelty, looked from one face to another. Then, after a long moment, in a voice quavering but deeply earnest, he said, "But I like you."

The singsong stopped before his earnestness. For a brief moment, it seemed as if his simple but gravely moving words would have some effect. Three of the boys looked at one another in uncertainty. They had been somehow touched.

But the bully had not been touched. "Go on home, Yellow!" he cried out again. And then to the gang, "Come on, fellers! Let's go!"

The game was begun again without the brown-haired Cowboy.

76

He looked desolately on for a minute or two, then turned and moved slowly away, following the frothing white line of the sea's edge, sadness in his drooping figure, bewilderment still on his sensitive face.

I watched him go. I felt profoundly sorry for him. It was as if I had just watched the stoning of a prophet.

He grew smaller in the distance. Still his words stayed with me.

"But I like you."

It is a long way from a mountain in Galilee to the beach at Malibu and today's world, yet that brown-haired boy, standing there on the sand, answering his young tormentors with an earnest declaration of his affection for them, vividly brought back to me those dramatic, revolutionary words, "But I say unto you, love your enemies. . . ."

He disappeared from my view around a wide sweep of the shore.

What would the years do to the little Cowboy? Could he go on saying to his enemies, "But I like you"? Could it ever be he would remain unspoiled in the world and one day be a saint?

Let's Break Bread

BY

GEORGE D. MARDIKIAN

FAMOUS SAN FRANCISCO RESTAURATEUR,
AUTHOR OF "SONG OF AMERICA"

"Man shall not live by bread alone."

—MATTHEW 4:4

TRULY AMERICA is the land of plenty. Her rich earth gives us the best and most nourishing food in the world, and this makes our children grow straight and tall and beautiful.

But sometimes, as I look at all this abundance, I wonder if we aren't taking it a little too much for granted. Aren't we forgetting, for instance, the Bible's reminder that "man shall not live by bread alone"—that food is more than just something to eat?

Perhaps the story of a simple Armenian custom will show you what I mean.

To Armenians, bread was veritably the staff of life. Many of them did not stay in one place and grow crops; they were eternally on the move. Without bread, baked from wheat they carried with them, they would have perished.

It was a sin to waste bread. If a crumb fell to the ground, the Armenian picked it up and kissed it, and said a prayer, and put it on a wall for the birds to eat.

Now, the traditional Armenian bread is lavash, a large round cracker that you break in your hands. And out of Armenian antiquity has come the custom of holding lavash over the dinner table with your guest, and breaking it together.

This means not only that you are each taking a piece of lavash to eat with your meal; it is your way of saying, "What is mine is yours." It means that you think so much of him that you are sharing with him the staff of your life, and thus the most precious thing you possess.

And it is done reverently, because you are also uniting in gratitude to God for the miracle of bread—and the even greater miracle of life.

So when I see the plenty around us, I wish that at every meal I could break bread with every one of you. Then together, in this old way, we could all say that we are brothers and could all thank God for our bountiful country.

To Be a Friend . . .

BY

ROBERT HARDY ANDREWS

NOVELIST AND MOTION PICTURE WRITER

"To do a little good is more than to accomplish great conquests."

—GAUTAMA BUDDHA

IN INDIA 2500 years ago, a man named Gautama Buddha walked the roads and preached and taught. His teachings are still remembered by five hundred million Buddhist believers in Asia and the Orient.

I am not a Buddhist. But I find no disloyalty to my faith in accepting advice as practical today as it was when Buddha first offered it. In a mango grove in Bihar he told one of his disciples that five things are necessary to achieve release from unhappiness and fear. These, he said, include: restraint, proper discourse, energy in producing good thoughts, firmness in pursuing them, and acquisition of true insight. But first of all, and above all, he said, the seeker must learn to be a good friend.

When people asked for a definition of friendliness, Buddha answered, "It means to have hope of the welfare of others more than for one's self. . . . It means affection unsullied by hope or thought of any reward on earth or in heaven."

Buddha admitted that such generous wholeheartedness would not be easy. Yet in the long run it is intensely practical. "Compassion and knowledge and virtue," he said, "are the only possessions that do not fade away."

"To be a good friend . . ." How simple it sounds—just five short words. Yet how much they represent! Think how much it could mean, a flowing out of new forces of friendship from person to person, and eventually from land to land.

Try as we may, there is no other form of security. As Buddha said, "Friendship is the only cure for hatred, the only guarantee of peace."

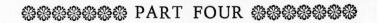 PART FOUR

Definitions
of Success

"Make no little plans; they have no magic to stir men's blood and probably themselves will not be realized. Make big plans; aim high in hope and work, remembering that a noble, logical diagram once recorded will never die, but long after we are gone will be a living thing, asserting itself with ever-growing insistency."

—DANIEL H. BURNHAM

THE GREATEST GOAL by Francis Steegmuller

RIDE YOUR HORSE! by George Seaton

CHANGE PACE! by William F. Knowland

BREAK THE RULES! by Edward D. Stone

THE GOLDEN BRACELET by George D. Mardikian

THE AIM by George N. Shuster

THE ART OF SUCCESS by Wilferd A. Peterson

The Greatest Goal

BY
FRANCIS STEEGMULLER

NOVELIST AND SHORT STORY WRITER,
AUTHOR OF
''FLAUBERT AND MADAME BOVARY''

"The principal thing in this world is to keep one's soul aloft."

—GUSTAVE FLAUBERT

GUSTAVE FLAUBERT, author of the great French novel *Madame Bovary*, was a very celebrated man, but in his conversation and his letters he always made a sharp—sometimes ferocious—distinction between mere fame and what he considered to be true accomplishment.

On one occasion, a literary lady who had recently won a prize wrote him that "these are the most glorious moments of my life—everyone is seeking me out to congratulate me and flatter me."

Flaubert replied severely: "The most glorious moments in your life are not the so-called days of success, but rather those days when out of dejection and despair, you feel rise in you a challenge to life, and the promise of future accomplishments." Then Flaubert gave his credo: the greatest goal in life, he said, is not the attainment of fame—"The principal thing in this world is to keep one's soul aloft."

Slaving away at writing the novels that are the expression of his own greatness, Flaubert never forgot that the fame they brought him was but the "outward sound" of the feeling he experienced on certain rare, exalted days when his soul was "aloft."

But this feeling is not the exclusive privilege of famous novelists. Service to the community, conscientious performance of one's job in the face of difficulties, careful guidance of one's children with a view to their best and most harmonious development—these and many other everyday duties hold the possibility of similarly deep gratification. For these activities one may receive and enjoy praise; but, just as in the case of Flaubert's art, the true satisfaction, the essence of success, comes not from the praise but from the doing.

Ride Your Horse!

BY

GEORGE SEATON

ACADEMY AWARD WINNING
MOTION PICTURE WRITER AND PRODUCER

"Don't let your horse ride you."

—OLD SAYING

IN THE CAVALRY, long ago, the drill sergeants had this advice for slack-wristed recruits: "Ride your horse!" they would shout—"Don't let your horse ride you!"

The same thing can be said about jobs. If you think of your job only as a means to an end—a pay check, a meal ticket—you're in for trouble. A successful worker is one who knows how to make his work really work for him.

This was brought home to me quite clearly many years ago in New York. It was during the depression and, in order to keep from starving, I went to work for a soap company. My job was as a member of a crew that went from door to door giving away samples of a new product.

Carrying a 30-pound case up and down the stairs of tenement houses was, to me, degrading and stultifying for a promising author. Worst of all, it left me so tired that I didn't have the energy to write my name.

One night I was describing my dull job to a friend of mine, a playwright, and he became ecstatic. The chance of talking to fifty or a hundred new and different people a day was truly exciting to him. He made me realize what I had been missing.

From that moment on, my job became a training ground for me as a writer. Each person who came to a door became a character to be studied and remembered—the mannerisms, the peculiarities of speech, the eccentricities of behavior. I couldn't wait to get home and jot down what I had seen and heard.

Eventually, I could tell from the way a door was opened whether there was a defeat in the apartment or hope. After a minute's conversation, I knew the nationality of the housewife and whether she hated her husband or loved him. I could guess whether she had a family or was childless. I learned to detect suspicion and fear in a voice and spot physical pain just from eyes.

So, whatever job you work at, make it work for you. There's hardly a career in the world that doesn't call for a knowledge of people. Whether you work in a parking lot, as receptionist in a dentist's office, a busboy, a gas station attendant, study the people you meet—learn to know them. It'll be well worth the effort.

Change Pace!

BY

WILLIAM F. KNOWLAND

FORMER SENATOR FROM CALIFORNIA

"Wisdom is knowing what to do next."
—SISTER MARY LAURETTA (*See page 163*)

EVEN IN his eighties, my father, a remarkable man, worked harder than most men half his age. He never gave up, he seldom slowed down. His sound personal advice was an inspiration to me all my life.

In my early activities I attempted to pattern my life at the pace he set for himself. I considered myself pretty busy as president of the Alameda High School student body, and with my studies to contend with, too, I had many problems on my mind. One evening I sighed and said: "It doesn't look as though I'll ever have time to relax and enjoy myself any more."

Dad came over and put his hand on my shoulder. "There is enjoyment in many things, son," he said. "Doing a good job is one of the best ways to find satisfaction that I know of. But remember this, Bill—there will come times when your only recreation will be a change of troubles."

Right away, my various jobs seemed less like problems and more like challenges. While deep in one task, I found relaxation in the thought of turning to something different. And once a job was done, I was relieved of unnecessary second thoughts about it because I was too busy doing something else.

Since then there have been many times when, recalling that advice, I've been able to push on to a new effort with renewed vitality. Often life seems arduous and demanding, but whenever I think of father's advice, I experience a lifting of the burdens and a sense of strength in "a change of troubles."

It has worked for me for many years. I think it can work for everyone.

Break the Rules!

BY

EDWARD D. STONE

FAMOUS ARCHITECT

"Whoso would be a man must be a non-conformist."
—RALPH WALDO EMERSON

SOME THIRTY-FIVE years ago, when I decided to be an architect, my older brother Hicks, who was also an architect, said to me that there were two attitudes that I must bring to the profession—singleness of purpose and an open mind. The first attitude—singleness of purpose—comes easily to anyone with an average amount of energy and ambition. But keeping an open mind is harder and much more important.

My brother pointed out that only with an open mind could one see all of the possible solutions to any problem. He cautioned against falling in love with your first idea and he warned me to beware of anyone who felt that there was only one solution. A dogmatic answer was the mark of a person with too few ideas. An open mind and flexibility in ideas avoided the impasse, and often an outsider's suggestion was the best.

This has been of immeasurable help to me. I have found it a governing rule for the conduct of my whole life. In passing judgment on architecture or people, I have tried to see if the positive attributes do not outmeasure the negative ones.

In this day and age, when the accusation of standardization in our country is so justified, Americans need to cultivate the open mind. We should encourage departure from the norm, and those who assert their individuality should find tolerance from their fellows.

Our lives would be enriched if each person's flights of fancy found receptive audiences and everyone was encouraged to be an individual. But let us not forget that he who dares to take a different path must first know where he's going.

The Golden Bracelet

BY

GEORGE D. MARDIKIAN

FAMOUS SAN FRANCISCO RESTAURATEUR,
AUTHOR OF ''SONG OF AMERICA''

"Keep your face to the sun and the shadows will fall behind."

—UNKNOWN

MY MOTHER had blue eyes and flaxen hair and her name was Haiganoush, and in accordance with the age-old wisdom of her people, she made sure that my brother Arshag and I each wore a *voski abaranchan*—a "golden bracelet."

Most Armenian mothers wanted their sons to have a "golden bracelet." By this they meant, not a piece of real jewelry, but a trade, a craft, a special ability. No matter where their sons went or what they did in life, they would always have it to fall back on. They could lose or be deprived of everything else, but their *voski abaranchan* would see them through.

Some boys learned carpentry, pottery or rug weaving. Arshag learned how to be a cobbler. Eventually, when he went to America, his first job was making boots. Later he became a restaurant manager, but it always gave him confidence and a sense of independence to know that, if need be, he could go back to his cobbler's bench.

As for me, I learned how to cook. This made my mother very happy, for she was sure then that I, as well as Arshag, wore a golden bracelet. I haven't worked at it for some time but cooking is like swimming or riding a bicycle. Once you learn, you never forget how to do it.

But all these years, I have kept a secret. My golden bracelet is not cooking at all. It is the quotation above, which I read a long time ago, when I first came to America.

Friends often wonder how I smile and stay cheerful, even when things don't seem to be going very well. I tell them it's because I think people are wonderful, and life is wonderful, and America is a wonderful, beautiful country. But most of all, it's because I've learned the meaning of those simple words. What they are saying is this: Turn your heart toward the radiance and warmth of God's love—and doubts, fears and unhappiness will disappear.

He who walks in God's light, and trusts in this miracle, will wear a golden bracelet every moment of every day, for the rest of his life. And perhaps even longer than that.

The Aim

BY

GEORGE N. SHUSTER

NOTED EDUCATOR,
NOTRE DAME UNIVERSITY

*"As for myself, I want to do my work well . . . and
to die well."*

—UNKNOWN FRENCH GIRL

IN 1919, I lived in Poitiers as a student in a room looking out
on the old street up which Jeanne d'Arc had come to see the
Dauphin. Like many a soldier just out of the trenches, I
thought of the place I had to make for myself in the world
rather than of how I would go about it or why. Early one
morning I overheard two girls talking on their way to work.
"As for myself," I heard one say, "I want to do my work
well . . . and to die well."

"To want to do one's work well." When you really want

to do something well, whatever it may be, you can laugh, sing, drink a toast to life.

But that is only part of it; now think of the business of living as ending with a balance sheet to be looked at when the business is over. Mortality's best prelude to immortality would be to find nothing in life of which one had to be terribly ashamed: to be sure no other human being could justly say you had ruined his spirit or grossly betrayed his trust, and even to be able to say that enemies had not been hated. In the conversation of the two French girls I found the conviction that life must retain a quality only the word *holiness* can describe. And I began to think of what my story would read like at the end.

I have not managed as well as the French girl doubtless did. Even so, it has been increasingly evident that our human society prospers only when there are many who see life as she did. Her sermon was brief, but it still seems to me the best I have ever heard.

The Art of Success

BY

WILFERD A. PETERSON

AUTHOR OF "THE ART OF LIVING"

"Do not pray for tasks equal to your powers. Pray for powers equal to your tasks."

—PHILLIPS BROOKS

EDITOR'S NOTE: *This is one of a series of brief essays* "The Art of Living," *which appeared recently on* Week's *"Words to Live By" page. Their popularity w* great that they have now been republished as a separate *ume by Simon and Schuster. Mr. Peterson is creative di of an advertising agency in Grand Rapids, Michigan.*

THERE ARE no secrets of success. Success is d things you know you should do. Success is not things you know you should not do.

Success is not limited to any one area of your

compasses all of the facets of your relationships: as parent, as wife or husband, as citizen, neighbor, worker and all of the others.

Success is not confined to any one part of your personality but is related to the development of all the parts: body, mind, heart and spirit. It is making the most of your total self.

Success is discovering your best talents, skills and abilities and applying them where they will make the most effective contribution to your fellow men.

Success is focusing the full power of all you are on what you have a burning desire to achieve.

Success is ninety-nine per cent mental attitude. It calls for love, joy, optimism, confidence, serenity, poise, faith, courage, cheerfulness, imagination, initiative, tolerance, honesty, humility, patience and enthusiasm.

Success is not arriving at the summit of a mountain as a final destination. It is a continuing upward spiral of progress. It is perpetual growth.

Success is having the courage to meet failure without being defeated. It is refusing to let present loss interfere with your long-range goal.

Success is accepting the challenge of the difficult. In the inspiring words of Phillips Brooks: "Do not pray for tasks equal to your powers. Pray for powers equal to your tasks. Then the doing of your work shall be no miracle, but you shall be the miracle."

PART FIVE

On Keeping Calm

"I still find each day too short for all the thoughts I want to think, all the walks I want to take, all the books I want to read, and all the friends I want to see. The longer I live the more my mind dwells upon the beauty and the wonder of the world."
—JOHN BURROUGHS

WHAT THE MOUNTAINS TAUGHT ME
by Justice William O. Douglas
LOOK UP! by Joseph Wood Krutch
BELIEVE AND ADORE! by Louise Dickinson Rich
ON ANIMALS by Fairfield Osborn
ON CHILLS AND THRILLS by Alfred Hitchcock
LET'S BE LAZY by Allen Churchill
"UNFINISHED BUSINESS" by Donald Culross Peattie

What the Mountains Taught Me

BY

WILLIAM O. DOUGLAS

ASSOCIATE JUSTICE,
UNITED STATES SUPREME COURT
AUTHOR OF "WEST OF THE INDUS"

"On every mountain height is rest."

—GOETHE

THE WOODS and streams of America . . . the ridges where deer graze . . . the high meadows where grass and shrubs hold back floods . . . gnarled trees on wind-blown points . . . lakes where loons call . . . thickets where quail flourish, sunsets and sunrises over glacier peaks—all these are bits of the wilderness we still possess.

They give us a retreat from the din of civilization; they are places of solitude where we can get rid of the tensions of modern life. They provide trails and campsites where we can rediscover the earth of which we are an integral part. They offer stately cathedrals where we can commune with God.

Look Up!

BY

JOSEPH WOOD KRUTCH

AUTHOR AND NATURALIST

"He who knows what sweets and virtues are in the ground, the waters, the plants, the heavens, and how to come at these enchantments, is the rich and royal man."

—RALPH WALDO EMERSON

MANY TAKE it for granted that progress means the gradual elimination of everything which God and nature put into our world and the substitution for it of the conveniences which man has made.

I like many of them well enough myself, and I have no illusions concerning the "noble savage." Civilized life is the only truly human life. I will take wild flowers and television if I can have them both. But a civilization which has no appreciation of or love for the beauties of nature is only a new kind of barbarism.

It is good that we have our parks, our museums, our nature-study clubs. Nevertheless, opportunities to see wild birds in flight or a wild flower blooming in lonely loveliness grow fewer and fewer because we do not value them enough.

Of course, we need paved highways. But we need quiet wood roads, too. We need television, yet we also need the opportunity to see geese flying against the autumn sky. Unless we realize how much we need these simple pleasures, the time may come when we won't have them. "Nature is the art of God," and a flower is more wonderful than the most ingenious of man's machines.

Believe and Adore!

BY
LOUISE DICKINSON RICH

AUTHOR OF "WE TOOK TO THE WOODS"

"If the stars should appear one night in a thousand years, how men would believe and adore; and preserve for many generations the remembrance of the City of God which has been shown!"

—RALPH WALDO EMERSON

WHEN WE WERE YOUNG, each one of us, the world was a place of wonder. Almost every hour brought adventure and discovery; so that the diary of a child might read: "On this day I saw a field of daisies, white and gold beneath the sun," or "Today I learned that water always runs down hill," or "My baby sister opened her eyes and looked at me this morning. She knew me."

As children, we stood amazed before beauty and natural

law and human fellowship, before the miracle of a seed's sprouting, of a snowflake's immutable hexagonal, of being able to read, so that unknown people spoke to us on paper. Everything was new and astonishing, from the busyness of ants about their hill, to the smile of a friend, to the certainty of God's concern with our well-being.

We could not remain children forever. It was neither possible nor desirable that we should. A part of the marvel of life is growth and development. But in growing up, we never cease to need the world of wonder. I remember a time when my whole existence fell to pieces around me, and I moved in hopeless chaos. Then one day a hummingbird flashed across my vision, a tiny living jewel hovering in the throat of a lemon lily. Suddenly I saw that the sun shone, that a gentle breeze stirred the tops of the trees, that the world of order and wonder was still there.

Somewhere a child laughed, and I found that I too could laugh again, and believe and adore. The stars were again in my sky; and I shall preserve for the rest of my life the remembrance of God's world which I had been shown.

On Animals

BY

FAIRFIELD OSBORN

PRESIDENT, NEW YORK
ZOOLOGICAL SOCIETY

*"I think I could turn and live with animals,
they are so placid and self-contain'd,
I stand and look at them long and long."*

—WALT WHITMAN

THESE ARE definitely words to live by for all people who
are fond of animals.

I was reminded of them some years back during the heat
of the Suez Canal crisis while talking with an official of a
large corporation that had interests in the Middle East.

"I guess you've got your problems," I remarked.

"We certainly have," he retorted, and went on to speak

of the damage that had occurred to some of their properties and the threat of further difficulties.

Then he added, "About the most cheering thing I've seen in the newspapers these last few days was the picture of that okapi that the Bronx Zoo just got from the Congo government. That gave me a real lift. It sounds crazy, but I remember thinking to myself, 'Well, I guess maybe the world's still all right, after all!'"

Of course my friend did not mean that there is anything all right about the problems in the Middle East or the Congo or any of the other difficulties our world is living through, but his remark implied that we need not get hysterical about them. We can certainly all agree that troubles are best and most easily solved when we approach them calmly.

This attitude, it seems to me, is one of the many boons we can gain from observing animals. If we look at them "long and long," we become conscious of the infinitely mysterious processes that, through the ages, have created all living things on this earth—including "even me."

With such a realization, immediate problems come into better perspective. Who can deny that this is the beginning of wisdom?

On Chills and Thrills

BY

ALFRED HITCHCOCK

HOLLYWOOD AND TV MASTER OF SUSPENSE

"A tale which holdeth children from play and old men from the chimney-corner."
—SIR PHILIP SIDNEY

THE OTHER DAY a fascinating statistic was brought to my notice. I was asked to believe that in a single year some 40,000,000 prescriptions will have been written for tranquilizers to relieve the tensions of the world Americans live in. Now, I have no quarrel with any sort of medication. But I believe I have a more pleasing prescription:

Take a suspense story . . . quake well . . . and keep quaking!

From the days when legends of bold deeds and sudden

death were sung by minstrels, the suspense story has enraptured audiences and made them forget for a little while the problems of their own lives. To hold a man spellbound for an hour is to return him refreshed to face tomorrow.

Of course the world of the suspense story is a world of make-believe. Of course it is what the critics call "escape." But is that bad? These are entertainments, designed to take you out of yourself, to make you believe while you read, or look at a screen, in the reality of what is there. When it is over, when the criminal is properly trapped and you are returned to your private worries, you find that your little excursion has made your mind clearer, your nerves calmer, your problems somehow easier to attack.

For some troubled persons I have no doubt that the siesta on the psychiatrist's couch is a necessity. But for a good many others who are disturbed by tension, my magic potion can have a healing effect.

This little homily is designed to free you of any guilty conscience from indulging in the pure entertainment of a suspense story. You may relax and enjoy the chills and thrills. As a tension reliever, they are just what the doctor ordered. And if they help you to be a calmer, better, happier person, then I shall feel that my labors in the field of crime have not altogether been in vain.

Let's Be Lazy

BY

ALLEN CHURCHILL

AUTHOR OF "THEY NEVER CAME BACK"

"Every man is as lazy as he dares to be."

—RALPH WALDO EMERSON

LAZINESS is disappearing from our lives. Give it the word test. How long has it been since you have heard someone say, "Trouble with him is, he's bone-lazy"?

I am not going to tell you that laziness is the road to happiness. Emerson, in the quotation above, doesn't either. Even so, he sensed what we all know now—that a man who has the courage, occasionally, to take time out of his life to stop and do nothing, and enjoy it, must have a deep confidence in himself, the future, and in whatever god he chooses to

111

worship. I envy the man propped up against a tree, waiting for a nibble on his line.

Why? Because I think he's got precisely what so many of us lack. The person with the courage to be lazy from time to time is not only confident, but realizes the necessity of assimilating daily experience, giving emotional energies a rest, and utilizing personal wisdom. It may sound like a paradox, but I truly believe that a man works best who has learned to loaf.

"Unfinished Business"

BY

DONALD CULROSS PEATTIE

AUTHOR AND NATURALIST

"I leave a great deal to 'unfinished business.'"

—ROBERT FROST

I SUPPOSE everyone who has been privileged to talk a while with Robert Frost has come away treasuring a memory of conversation fruity with wisdom. After such an hour with the great but easy old poet, beside the hearth at his Vermont farm, I found the casual words above to linger longest in my thoughts.

Roll them about in your mind, you worried and hurried ones! Savor the richness of time and patience, of hope and faith, that lies in this simple utterance. For there is much in the business of our lives that we cannot hasten, for all the

113

urgency of speed that today bedevils us. There is much—
and this is true of the most important of our affairs—that
cannot be concluded in a day, or a week, or a month, but
must be let to take a guided course. We are too prone to
bring problems with us to our rest, and thrash them over
uselessly. So I, for one, over and over, give thanks for the
slyly sensible remark by Robert Frost.

He was, when I come to think of it, living as nature lives.
When an acorn fallen from an oak at last splits husk, sprouts,
and begins to take root, how much unfinished business lies
ahead of it! It has no contract with the sun and rain to have
become an oak tree by a certain date. But with their help it
will grow until it towers and spreads shade, in the good time
we call God's.

We ought as trustingly to let our plans and problems
ripen to solution, knowing there is another Hand in the business beside our own. To leave a question to "unfinished
business" is not to abandon the task. It is to attain the serenity which will give us strength to carry on with it when the
call to effort comes.

PART SIX

Space Age Speaking

"The destiny of mankind is not decided by material computation. When great causes are on the move in the world . . . we learn that we are spirits, not animals, and that something is going on in space and time, and beyond space and time, which, whether we like it or not, spells duty."

—WINSTON CHURCHILL

A GENERAL LOOKS AT GOD
by Major General John B. Medaris

WHY I BELIEVE IN IMMORTALITY
by Wernher von Braun

ON CHARACTER
by Lieutenant General Arthur G. Trudeau

THE VISION by Arthur C. Clarke

BEYOND THE STARS by Howard Van Smith

Space Age
Speaking

A General Looks at God

BY

MAJOR GENERAL
JOHN B. MEDARIS, U.S.A. (RET.)

FORMER COMMANDING GENERAL,
U.S. ARMY ORDNANCE MISSILE COMMAND

*"The Universe is centered on neither the Earth nor
the Sun—it is centered on God."*
—ALFRED NOYES

IN THIS BUSY AGE, in these days of intense scientific
activity as we approach the conquest of space, it is not surprising that we find ourselves restless, unfulfilled, unsatisfied.

Amidst all this kaleidoscopic movement the inner soul
of man must find an eternal harbor, some home port that
will stay put, his own internal haven of peace. When he
fails to find such an anchorage his mind refuses the challenge
of change. Mental illness becomes an epidemic of the times.

And youth, cast afloat on uncharted seas, lacks assurance.
The cry of pain and insecurity rises from the hearts of the

untrained—"Where am I?" . . . "Where am I going?" . . . "Who and where is the authority?" And the world is too busy to answer.

Yet the answer is there, the answer without which man becomes a scurrying animal without purpose or direction, fighting for the next morsel of food.

The answer is in the majestic order of the universe and its obedience to unchanging law.

The answer is there—in the certainty and regularity of the seasons, in the march of the sun, the moon, and the stars, in the regular coming of night and day, in the balance between man's consumption of life-giving oxygen and its production by the plant life of the earth, in the regularity of change from the barren silence of winter to the greening, growing life of spring, in the cry of a newborn child with its ever-new demonstration of the miracle of life.

This timeless, changeless order is an assurance of unchallenged authority, a sign of safe anchorage for the troubled spirit of man.

Increase in man's knowledge does not mean the discovery of new things, but only the extension of his understanding and ability to use that which already is, and has always been. Like the growth of a child from infant to adult, man is "discovering" worlds new to him—but old to God.

When this is fully realized, man can stand straight and tall, assured in the face of apparent uncertainty, secure in his knowledge of the way home, at peace with himself because he is at peace with Almighty God.

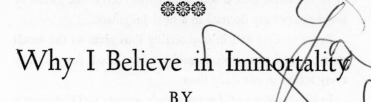

Why I Believe in Immortality

BY

WERNHER VON BRAUN

INVENTOR AND SPACE EXPERT

"I believe . . . that the soul of Man is immortal and will be treated with justice in another life respecting its conduct in this."

—BENJAMIN FRANKLIN

TODAY, more than ever before, our survival—yours and mine and our children's—depends on our adherence to ethical principles. Ethics alone will decide whether atomic energy will be an earthly blessing or the source of mankind's utter destruction.

Where does the desire for ethical action come from? What makes us want to be ethical? I believe there are two forces which move us. One is belief in a Last Judgment, when every one of us has to account for what we did with God's great gift of life on the earth. The other is belief in an immortal soul, a soul which will cherish the award or suffer the penalty decreed in a final Judgment.

Belief in God and in immortality thus gives us the moral strength and the ethical guidance we need for virtually every action in our daily lives.

In our modern world many people seem to feel that science has somehow made such "religious ideas" untimely or old-fashioned.

But I think science has a real surprise for the skeptics. Science, for instance, tells us that nothing in nature, not even the tiniest particle, can disappear without a trace.

Think about that for a moment. Once you do, your thoughts about life will never be the same.

Science has found that nothing can disappear without a trace. Nature does not know extinction. All it knows is transformation!

Now, if God applies this fundamental principle to the most minute and insignificant parts of His universe, doesn't it make sense to assume that He applies it also to the masterpiece of His creation—the human soul? I think it does. And everything science has taught me—and continues to teach me—strengthens my belief in the continuity of our spiritual existence after death. Nothing disappears without a trace.

On Character

BY

LIEUTENANT GENERAL ARTHUR G. TRUDEAU

CHIEF OF RESEARCH AND DEVELOPMENT, U.S. ARMY

"Master yourself and you can master anything."

—PROVERB

AS CHIEF of Research and Development for the Army, I meet with great numbers of scientists every day. Many of them are Ph.D.'s—Doctors of Philosophy in various special fields. Ph.D.'s are among the finest brains and the most congenial people I have ever dealt with. So I hope they will forgive me when I say that what this country needs—and needs badly—are more Ch.D.'s—Doctors of Character.

Not everyone can be a Ph.D., but every one of us *can* be

a Ch.D. And I, for one, would like to see all of us strive to be just that. If there is one attribute that needs more thought, more attention, in these troublesome times it is sound character and adherence to the moral principles that were the trademark of our forefathers.

Man has now unleashed nuclear energy. He has placed artificial satellites around the earth and around our daystar, the sun.

We can move mountains. We can change the course of rivers. We can bounce radio signals off the moon. The pace of scientific advancement is continually accelerating.

But there is one thing which science cannot create—and I hope it never will—and that is character. Character is something each one of us must build for himself, out of the laws of God and nature, the examples of others, and—most of all—out of the trials and errors of daily life. Character is the total of thousands of small daily strivings to live up to the best that is in us. Character is the final decision to reject whatever is demeaning to oneself or to others and with confidence and honesty to choose the right.

Once you make that final choice, you will unleash within yourself a power more rewarding and greater than any nuclear energy—the power of a life firmly grounded on discipline, courage, honor, faith, and love. These are the qualities on which the future of our world depends.

The Vision

BY

ARTHUR C. CLARKE

FORMER CHAIRMAN OF THE BRITISH
INTERPLANETARY SOCIETY,
AUTHOR OF "THE EXPLORATION OF SPACE"

"God lead us past the setting of the sun
To wizard islands, of august surprise;
God make our blunders wise."

—VACHEL LINDSAY

NOT LONG AGO, I was in Barcelona attending a meeting of the International Astronautical Federation. One evening I was walking with a fellow delegate, an officer from the U. S. Air Force Office of Scientific Research. We were talking about the future and the learned papers about outer space we had been hearing that day.

Suddenly my friend paused and pointed. High above us, on a tall column, was a statue of Christopher Columbus,

123

staring out toward the horizon. As he looked up at the great navigator my friend reminded me of a piece of history long forgotten which we would all do well to remember.

Five hundred years ago Venice was the mistress of the seas—the unchallenged ruler of the maritime world. Then explorers began looking westward, and to Venice came men with dreams, men who believed that they could find new trade routes across the Western ocean. But the doges were not interested; for centuries the commerce of half the world had paid them tribute—why should they be bothered with wild adventures in unknown seas? They made their choice. They chose to stay with the old and comfortable ways of doing things.

So the explorers sought and found encouragement elsewhere. Almost within a generation the riches of the New World were pouring into the coffers of Spain and Portugal. The tide of wealth and power ebbed from Venice, never to return.

The lesson of this is plain for all of us to see. Many are aware of it. But do we fully realize the finality of the challenge which now confronts the Western world?

Today the Age of Space reaches out to touch every home, every schoolroom, every village everywhere. We shall not survive if we are lazy, soft, or complacent. I do not mean that we are blind, as the doges of Venice were. But we shall be half blind if we do not pursue the challenge fully. The choice is clear, not only for our leaders, but for every one of us: We choose between greatness—and oblivion.

Beyond the Stars

BY

HOWARD VAN SMITH

PULITZER PRIZE REPORTER

"Beyond the stars—what?
Is it the beginning or end you see?
For beyond the stars—what?"

—ANONYMOUS

I WAS sitting on the lawn of my Miami home with a friend one night recently. He was something of an astronomer. He didn't have any degrees, and he didn't belong to any of the amateur astronomy clubs which are so popular in this area. But he had spent several years at sea and had become familiar with the names of the stars and constellations.

He was naming them—Orion and the Great Bear—as if they were old friends.

Sailors, he explained, often sit on deck at night and think about the stars.

"Did you ever think of infinity?" he asked me.

"Why, yes, of course," I replied. "I guess everyone does. You mean, well, endlessness?"

"I mean," he said, "did you ever look up there and see the physical proof of that endlessness?"

I hadn't. I had thought there were millions of stars, some that I could see and some that could be seen only through the giant telescopes. And I thought, too, that space reached out beyond comprehension and perhaps that there were millions more stars and planets still to be recorded.

"But you can see infinity, or at least the idea of it," he said.

"How?" I wanted to know.

"Well, then look," he said. "You don't even need a telescope."

I stared up into the vast sky.

"You still don't understand?" he asked.

"It looks endless. I see that."

"Now you are beginning to see it," he said. "Suppose your eyes were suddenly so powerful you could see every known and recorded star. Say you are looking at the farthest star or constellation known. Could you call that the end?"

I kept looking up and waited for him to continue.

"Then suppose after the last star there was a wall or some kind of enclosure," he went on. "I mean just theoretically. But on the other side of it wouldn't there have to be more space? Build another wall farther out and the same thing would have to happen again. You see, it's impossible for it to end. There always has to be space beyond, no matter how many times you do it. It has to be infinity, something without end."

I looked into the sky, and beyond. It was too great to comprehend—it was infinity. I understood what philosophers mean when they say the infinite is God.

The World Within

"Among all my patients in the second half of life . . . every one of them fell ill because he had lost what the living religions of every age have given their followers, and none of them has been really healed who did not regain his religious outlook."

—CARL G. JUNG

Why Men Survive

BY

LAURENCE M. GOULD

PRESIDENT OF CARLETON COLLEGE

"Where there is no vision, the people perish."

—PROVERBS 29:18

I DO NOT BELIEVE the greatest threat to our future is from bombs or guided missiles. I don't think our civilization will die that way. I think it will die when we no longer care —when the spiritual forces that make us wish to be right and noble die in the hearts of men.

Arnold Toynbee has pointed out that 19 of 21 notable civilizations died from within and not by conquest from without. There were no bands playing and no flags waving when these civilizations decayed; it happened slowly, in the quiet and dark when no one was aware.

If America is to grow great, we must stop gagging at the word "spiritual." Our task is to rediscover and reassert our faith in the spiritual, nonutilitarian values on which American life has really rested from its beginning.

Robert Frost's Secret

BY

CHARLES W. COLE

PRESIDENT-EMERITUS
OF AMHERST COLLEGE

"The best thing that we're put here for's to see."

—ROBERT FROST

WHEN ROBERT FROST was a freshman in college, his fraternity brothers worried about him because he took long walks alone in the woods. Finally a delegation of seniors waited on him and after some fumbling preliminaries one asked, "Frost, what do you do walking by yourself in the woods?"

Freshman Frost looked at them and replied, "Gnaw bark." Thereafter they left him alone.

Actually what Frost was doing in the woods was meditating. He still takes long walks and he still meditates. In part, it is his ability to do so which makes him America's greatest living poet.

There is one kind of meditation which is passive, a quiet sinking into the self, a sort of contemplation. But with most of us, what passes for thought is a purposeless stream of consciousness, like an uncut motion picture with our own confused inner dialogue attached.

Robert Frost's kind of meditation is neither passive nor meaningless. It is directed, tenacious and purposeful. He is able to take a word, or an idea, and hold his mind to it while he looks it over from all angles, turns it inside out, dissects it. By doing so, he sees new aspects, new meanings, new beauties, even in tired and time-worn phrases.

It is such meditating that produces insight into people and a knowledge of the world we live in.

Why not try it? Pick some word or idea and really hold your mind to it. If we all could learn to meditate in this constructive manner for just ten or fifteen minutes a day, we would become more exciting people to live with, more tolerant of others, more helpful to them. We would have achieved understanding, and understanding begets sympathy.

One Thing at a Time

BY

EDDIE ALBERT

MOTION PICTURE ACTOR AND PRODUCER

"Appreciate the moment."

—ISAMU NOGUCHI

I MET Isamu Noguchi, the American-born Japanese sculptor and designer, when I went to Japan in 1956 to make *The Teahouse of the August Moon.* At a time of tension, he gave me some advice which changed my whole life. In honesty, I use and enjoy it today with every breath I take.

The monsoon had caught us, darkening the skies with rain, holding up our picture six weeks. We were fatigued and depressed. I had seen little of the charm and beauty of Japan so, before we left, I asked Noguchi if he would show me something he considered lovely, and characteristic, maybe a Zen Buddhist Temple.

I expected this famous artist to reveal a sight special and exotic, something to marvel at. I was disappointed when he took me out in the country from Nara, a small town near Kyoto, and pointed to an old farmhouse. We entered a large bare room. There was no altar and no priest, no Oriental mystery. An incredibly old woman served us tea. I crouched on the hard floor, my knees hurting, as she brought one thing at a time—a bowl, a copper pot, a tray and so on. We went through the traditional formal ceremonies.

"Now shall we appreciate the utensils?" Noguchi asked. An odd remark! But he went on: "The ceremony was to slow you down with one thing at a time. What you must learn is to appreciate the moment."

He picked up a bowl that had been in front of me for half an hour. I had not really looked at it. Now, as Noguchi turned it in his hands, I saw it for the first time. It was delightfully curved, glowing with a rich gold patina. Then Noguchi motioned toward a slim vase containing three delicate flowers, artfully arranged. I had taken them for granted.

"One thing at a time," Noguchi repeated gently. "Appreciate the moment."

My depression vanished. Ever since then, I have found life exhilarating wherever I am, even in times of stress.

It was strange that an American like me had to go to Japan to learn how to live. But I think I appreciate that moment with Noguchi more than any other in my life—except, of course, this wonderful moment of being alive and knowing it *right now.*

On Meditation

BY

DR. R. W. LUXTON

NOTED PHYSICIAN

"In quietness . . . shall be your strength."

—ISAIAH 30:15

I CANNOT OVERSTATE the importance of the habit of quiet meditation for health of body, mind and spirit. Modern man's life is grossly abnormal. Our days are spent in continuous activity and our senses stimulated incessantly, so that we have neither time nor opportunity for quiet.

We search for the Kingdom of Heaven in every quarter except where we are told on excellent authority that it happens to be—*within us.* We need to meditate daily on great truths. We need to explore our own lives, our motives, our plans, in the clear light God provides as we sit quietly and unhurriedly in His Presence.

Find Strength in Silence

BY

HOWARD VAN SMITH

PULITZER PRIZE REPORTER

"To be alone with Silence is to be alone with God."
—SAMUEL MILLER HAGEMAN

A FRIEND of mine, a man in his late fifties, has such a benign calmness about him that just being with him brings a feeling of peace. One day I asked him how, in a world of rushed and harried people, he maintained such evenness of disposition.

"I've been asked that before," he said, "and I believe I confused my questioner. My answer was 'silence.' I find it's the greatest refresher there is."

I wasn't surprised, for I hadn't expected an ordinary answer. But how could anyone put silence to work?

"You simply enjoy it," he said with a smile. "Usually the senses are bringing so much sight, sound and so many other things to us that they occupy most of our time. But to sit in silence now and then, with the outside world withheld, means to cut all this off and free the mind so that it can become itself."

"You mean all you do is just sit still and think?"

"No, not exactly," he said. "You see, thinking, using words, is an echo of sound. I mean detaching the mind from all outside activity so that, in a sense, there is nothing there but itself."

I smiled too, but I feared he had carried me along now beyond my depth.

"What comes to you when you do this?" I asked.

"Why, peace, repose—there's a great deal of power in this kind of silence. But I wouldn't try to describe it. The only answer is for you to try it yourself."

Since then I have followed his advice. It wasn't so easy at first—detaching the mind from all the outside activity that usually controls it—but I wouldn't trade this practice now for anything in the world. I've been surprised too to learn how many others do it. Some businessmen close the doors of their offices for five minutes at a certain time each day. They say there comes a calming away of the daily strain which nothing else can bring.

What is this wonderful power of silence?

I agree with my friend when he said he would not try to

describe it. But one result is a moment's conserving of the bodily and mental forces we so easily waste. And sometimes too I think you gain a new sense of being, that you learn to know that still part of you that lies behind all life's activities, that quiet consciousness that is forever yourself.

But, as my friend said, the only way to know the peace this brings is to try it yourself.

A Religious Experience

BY

ROLAND GAMMON

AUTHOR AND LECTURER

"Life, like a dome of many-colored glass,
Stains the white radiance of eternity."

—SHELLEY

YEARS AGO, as a boy in Maine, I stood in the May moonlight beside a glistening lake. Suddenly, in the forest quiet as I watched the moon-silvered waves and heard the winds stir the tall pines, the solitary scene dissolved in an ocean of light.

Behind, beneath and above—indeed, bursting from trees, thicket, flowers, stones, waves and star-clad sky—glowed a light which enveloped and dissolved me in its beauty. A heart-piercing joy lifted me up; a tremendous new felicity

141

thrilled my being even as it confirmed my youthful yearning for what the saints call "union with God."

In that silent opening I knew the universe was a living, luminous emanation of God himself; that His continuous, creative Presence sustained every field, flower, flake, scatter of stars and miracle of life and that, if and when that Presence should ever be withdrawn, the world would vanish; that, as the prophets and poets had foretold, every human being was the individualized embodiment of divine Being and that the whole purpose of life was to realize that divinity here and now.

The Bridge

BY

OLIVER LA FARGE

PULITZER PRIZE NOVELIST
AND ANTHROPOLOGIST

"We are all in this life together."

—SAYING

"WE ARE ALL in this life together," I heard a Quaker say
once. "What happens to one happens to all."

His words crystallized my own vague feelings and started
me thinking about the Divine Spirit which is present in
all men. It is not only in yourself, but in people of all races,
in your enemies and in your friends. It means that no one
is hopeless, no one beneath contempt.

It is hard to keep this realization always in mind. But when
I remember it, I see that it is a bridge—for if no man is an

island, it is also true that men often dig moats around themselves which cannot be crossed by habitual smiles or the glib use of first names. Good will, friendliness, scientific knowledge are not enough to reach across the chasms between people, between races and cultures. We have to remember—constantly—that there is a divine spark in all of us; we are all in this life together.

Island of Peace

BY

ILEANA

PRINCESS OF RUMANIA

"The wise man looks inside his heart and finds eternal peace."

—OLD SAYING

AN ISLAND of peace and quiet is greatly longed for, both materially and spiritually, in this world of turmoil and unrest.

Few of us ever find this haven—or even have an idea of how to start searching for it. Some of us have taken trips around the world; others have climbed high mountains, or sailed on lonely seas. We are divided into two categories of people: those of us who are trying to escape from something, and those of us who are trying to find something.

It would be difficult for many of us to define what that

145

something is. But in any event, movement alone is not enough. To run away is vain effort, for we can leave behind neither ourselves nor the persistent call of God. As in the words of David:

"Whither shall I go from thy spirit? or whither shall I flee
from thy presence?
If I ascend up into heaven, thou art there: if I make my bed
in hell, behold, thou art there.
If I take the wings of the morning, and dwell in the uttermost
parts of the sea;
Even there shall thy hand lead me. . . ."

I have no doubt that our unrest is due to an unrecognized hunger for God, which will not be denied. Spiritual search is often replaced by high adventure; far horizons beckon us to find what is, after all, within our own souls—God.

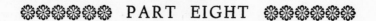

PART EIGHT

Look to This Day

"Only one person in a thousand knows the trick of really living in the present."

—STORM JAMESON

❀❀❀

Look to This Day

EDITOR'S NOTE: *A* This Week *reader suggested these "Words to Live By." The poem, sometimes known as "Salutation of the Dawn," has been attributed to the ancient Hindus, but scholars believe it to be of more recent origin.*

LOOK TO this day,
For it is life, the very life of life.
In its brief course lie all the verities and realities of your
existence:
The glory of action,
The bliss of growth,
The splendor of beauty,
For yesterday is but a dream and tomorrow is only a vision;
But today well lived makes every yesterday a dream of
happiness, and every tomorrow a vision of hope.
Look well, therefore, to this day.

"Oh, Those Days of Childhood!"

BY

GRANDMA MOSES

ARTIST AND CENTENARIAN

"Happiness follows simplicity."

—IRISH PROVERB

EDITOR'S NOTE: *This is from* Grandma Moses, My Life's History, *edited by Otto Kallir and published by Harper & Brothers.*

IN THE SPRINGTIME of life there is aplenty to do. Oh, those damp snowy days, early in spring, when we loved to go to the woods, and look for the first bloom of the trailing arbutus, which sometimes blooms beneath the snow, or gather the pussy willows. Feeling nearer to God's intentions, nearer to nature. Where in some respects, we are free, where

150

there is beauty and tranquillity, where we sometimes long to be, quiet and undisturbed, free from the hubbub of life.

Haying time on the farm, when they gather the grain, fruit and berries of all description, and the little folks gather the eggs. When the church picnic comes, and the children can have all the cake and lemonade they want, water melon and peanuts, what a wonderful treat!

And the fall of the year, and there are many odd jobs to attend to, food to be stored away for the coming cold weather, the ground to be plowed for rye and other crops before it is frozen hard. Ditches to dig. Poultry to cull and house.

Thanksgiven, in some homes there will be rejoicing, in others there will be sorrow. But we that can give thanks, should, there is so much to be thankful for, and praise God for all blessings, and the abundance of all things.

And then wintertime! When zero stands at 25 or 30, when we cannot deny the pleasure of skating till we have bumped heads, and bleedy noses, and the ice is like glass. Oh what joy and pleasure as we get together, to go for the Christmas tree, what aircastles we build as we slide down the hill, who can rebuild what we see on that Christmas tree?

Oh, those days of childhood!

Hour in the Sun

BY

JOHN H. BRADLEY

AUTHOR AND EDUCATOR

*". . . I was rich, if not in money, in sunny hours and
summer days. . . ."*

—HENRY DAVID THOREAU

WHEN THOREAU wrote that line he was thinking of the
Walden Pond he knew as a boy.

Woodchoppers and the Iron Horse had not yet greatly
damaged the beauty of its setting. A boy could go to the
pond and lie on his back against the seat of a boat, lazily
drifting from shore to shore while the loons dived and the
swallows dipped around him. Thoreau loved to recall such
sunny hours and summer days "when idleness was the most
attractive and productive business."

I too was once a boy in love with a pond, rich in sunny hours and summer days. Sun and summer are still what they always were, but the boy and the pond changed. The boy, who is now a man, no longer finds much time for idle drifting. The pond has been annexed by a great city. The swamps where herons once hunted are now drained and filled with houses. The bay where water lilies quietly floated is now a harbor for motor boats. In short, everything that the boy loved no longer exists— except in the man's memory of it.

Some people insist that only today and tomorrow matter. But how much poorer we would be if we really lived by that rule! So much of what we do today is frivolous and futile and soon forgotten. So much of what we hope to do tomorrow never happens. The past is the bank in which we store our most valuable possessions: the memories that give meaning and depth to our lives.

Those who truly treasure the past will not bemoan the passing of the good old days, because days enshrined in memory are never lost. Death itself is powerless to still a remembered voice or erase a remembered smile. And for one boy who is now a man, there is a pond which neither time nor tide can change, where he can still spend a quiet hour in the sun.

The Good World

BY

ROBERT FONTAINE

AUTHOR OF "THE HAPPY TIME"
AND "MY UNCLE LOUIS"

"It is a very good world for the purposes for which
it was built; and that is all anything is good for."

—HENRY WARD BEECHER

ONCE, AS A SMALL BOY, I was convinced by a sidewalk prophet with a magnificent but dirty beard that the world was to end in 48 hours.

Knowledge of the world's end rather pleased me. I soon would stand with the angels on clouds of pink joy and do nothing but sing all day. I would say goodbye to homework to dentists, and to beating rugs in the back yard after school.

When, 48 hours later, the time had come and the world was still shining there, I was disappointed—at first. Then

I thought, It's not so bad after all, this world. We had the sky, the stars, the trees, hockey, basketball, love, the movies, Christmas, and picnics. They would surely do for a while.

This true story is also, of course, a small parable. A good many times in my life I have decided the world was a sorry place, badly managed. Each time I have so thought, the words of Mr. Beecher, quoted above, have come to mind. The words are so obviously true. The purpose of the world is not to provide us with constant bliss or aimless gaiety, but with opportunities to strengthen and develop our moral and spiritual selves.

It is a world that provides us with constant and ever-changing challenges to our faith, our courage and our dreams—and ever-changing opportunities to develop ourselves beyond our earth-bound beginnings.

Those are the purposes for which this very good world was, indeed, built and I find it difficult to deny that it serves these purposes in an admirable and breath-taking way.

Beyond the Sundown

BY

THOMAS HORNSBY FERRIL

POET

"Beyond the sundown is tomorrow's wisdom,
today is going to be long, long ago."

—THOMAS HORNSBY FERRIL

EDITOR'S NOTE: *Thomas Hornsby Ferril, of Denver, Colorado, has been called by Carl Sandburg "a poet, wit, historian, man of books and human affairs, and . . . terrifically and beautifully American." He recently won the first annual Robert Frost Poetry Prize. The lines at the opening of this selection are one of the nine inscriptions from Mr. Ferril's poetry in the rotunda of the Colorado State Capitol, Denver.*

I OFTEN ENJOY thinking about how people in the far-off future will look back on us with insatiable fascination, just as we look back on the ancient Egyptians, the Greeks, or the

Elizabethans. Despite terrifying global tensions, I believe that our times, in future retrospect, will be called a golden age.

And, if our ancestors could visit us today, what would they be saying of us? Make believe that Shakespeare has come back to ask what's going on in your own town. Let Newton and Galileo chat with that young physicist on your block. Take Leonardo to your airport, Hippocrates to your hospital. Hear them ask how any hour of history could be so miraculous as ours. Then ask your own heart if you deserve such marvels and how much you appreciate them.

Isn't today a day men will look back upon with amazement and envy? Seize it! Enjoy it! The most humdrum experiences can be charged with shining wonder if only we will look at them through eyes of other men at other times. We've lived on this planet for only the flick of an eyelash, and "now," as I suggested once in a poem, "is always beginning."

A Good Time to Be Alive

BY

EDGAR ANSEL MOWRER

AUTHOR, FOREIGN CORRESPONDENT,
PULITZER PRIZE WINNER

> *"This time, like all other times, is a very good one,*
> *if we but know what to do with it."*
>
> —RALPH WALDO EMERSON

I GREW UP in one of the most secure places and periods
that have ever existed, the American Middle West before
1914, and found it tedious. The older I grew, the less I
liked the tranquillity of it. The more I read, the more I reacted
against my oversecure environment: I regretted not having
lived in a more exciting place and age—Benvenuto Cellini's
Italy, perhaps, or Drake's Spanish Main, or the Paris of the
Three Musketeers. Those were the days! Oh, to have been
with Uncle Ethan on that Union gunboat at Vicksburg!

Then came 1914. World War I, the subsequent revolutions and famines, the world-wide economic depression, the sinister rise of Fascism and Nazism, and the holocaust of World War II—these transformed that secure environment into an all but incredible memory. Since 1914 excitement has been the rule, not the exception. Indeed, there has been so much tension that at times the crises, the bloodshed, cruelty and unending public pressures have made me wonder at my earlier restlessness. Almost I have longed for the boredom of my boyhood and sighed for the more stable, neater world of Jane Austen.

But never for long. For there is a challenge today that cannot but quicken the pulse. Ours is a good time to be alive. It is a time when anyone can, if he so chooses, find a kind of satisfaction rarely attainable—participation in a struggle for essential values.

No personal experience can be more thrilling than a supreme adventure of the human race. Our Western civilization is undergoing a decisive test . . . its leadership is challenged. In being called upon to face that challenge, Americans are confronted with unequaled opportunity.

Ahead of them lies the great assignment of preserving the best part and shaping a richer future. If man's deepest greatness is his capacity to choose, to suffer and to enjoy, then happy is the generation born, like ours, to take part in earth-shaking events.

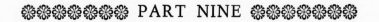

PART NINE

Ways of Life

A selection of tested rules for everyday living

WISDOM ON A BLACKBOARD by Sister Mary Lauretta
HOW TO BE A WINNER by Vernon Law
TEN WISE WISHES by Walter Reid Hunt
FORMULAS FOR FAME by Thomas A. Edison
ABRAHAM LINCOLN SAID selected by
Ralph G. Newman

Wisdom on a Blackboard

BY

SISTER MARY LAURETTA

TEACHER

EDITOR'S NOTE: *Sister Mary Lauretta, who teaches science at Columbus High School in Marshfield, Wisconsin (population 12,394), has won national fame as a teacher. Every year for five years she has produced a winner in the Westinghouse Science Talent Search. Her secret weapon: inspiration—often kindled by blackboard sayings which she changes every day. We asked her to select some of her favorites for* This Week, *and here is her answer:*

LIKE MOST TEACHERS I, too, have collected sayings and words that might give students motivating thoughts. For many of the would-be maxims I was unable to trace the author. That, however, does not destroy their intention.

163

Here are the maxims that appear most often on my classroom bulletin board:

1. What you don't know you can always learn.
2. Talk less, think more.
3. The real essence of work is concentration.
4. Every time you speak, your mind is on parade.
5. Every day gives you another chance.
6. Small minds discuss persons. Average minds discuss events. Great minds discuss ideas.
7. Wisdom is knowing what to do next.
8. The more you know, the more you know you ought to know.
9. Some men grow, others swell.
10. A thing done right today means no trouble tomorrow.
11. Not what you do, but how you do it.
12. It is thinking about the load that makes one tired.
13. Be ashamed to find yourself idle.
14. The first thing to do is to fall in love with your work.
15. Time waits for no one.
16. Men who do things that count never stop to count them.
17. Science reveals the secrets of God.

How to Be a Winner

BY

VERNON LAW

PITCHER FOR THE PITTSBURGH PIRATES

EDITOR'S NOTE: *Most major-league baseball pitchers keep a "little black book" in which they note weaknesses of opposing batters. Vernon Law, star of the Pittsburgh Pirates, has kept such a notebook for several years, but with a difference. Into Law's book, along with the usual baseball information, go shrewd observations that apply to life as well as baseball. Here are some examples:*

You'll never become a .300 hitter unless you take your bat off your shoulder.

•

When you start to slide—slide. He who changes his mind may exchange a good leg for a broken one.

•

A winner never quits and a quitter never wins.

•

Experience is a hard teacher because she gives the test first, the lesson afterwards.

•

Nobody ever became a ballplayer by walking after the ball.

•

If you don't play to win, why keep score?

•

There is no "I" in team.

•

Some people are so busy learning the tricks of the trade that they never learn the trade.

•

Don't throw the ball before you have it.

•

When you're through learning, you're through.

Ten Wise Wishes

BY

WALTER REID HUNT

MINISTER

EDITOR'S NOTE: *The late Dr. Walter Reid Hunt, a Unitarian minister of Duxbury, Massachusetts, called these his "Morning Wishes." They were suggested to* This Week *by reader Bernard S. Redmont.*

TODAY, I pray for—

1. A few friends who understand me and yet remain my friends.
2. Work to do which has real value, and without which the world would feel poorer.
3. An understanding heart.
4. Moments of leisure.
5. A mind unafraid to travel, even though the trail be not blazed.

6. A sight of the eternal hills and the unresting sea, and of something beautiful the hand of man has made.
7. The power to laugh.
8. Nothing at the expense of others.
9. The sense of the presence of God.
10. And the patience to wait for the coming of these things with the wisdom to know when they come.

Formulas for Fame

BY

THOMAS A. EDISON

INVENTOR AND GREAT AMERICAN

EDITOR'S NOTE: *In 1961, 30 years after his death, Thomas Alva Edison took his place in the celebrated Hall of Fame at New York University. Below are some "Words to Live By" from this distinctively American genius:*

There is far more opportunity than there is ability.

Education isn't play—and it can't be made to look like play. It is hard, hard work. But it can be made interesting work.

The stomach is the only part of man which can be fully satisfied. The yearning of man's brain for new knowledge and experience and for more pleasant and comfortable surroundings never can be completely met. It is an appetite which cannot be appeased.

*We shall have no better conditions in the future if we are
satisfied with all those which we have at present.*

Everything comes to him who hustles while he waits.

*The very first thing an executive must have is a fine mem-
ory. Of course it does not follow that a man with a fine
memory is necessarily a fine executive. But if he has the
memory he has the first qualification, and if he has not the
memory nothing else matters.*

Restlessness is discontent and discontent is the first necessity of progress. Show me a thoroughly satisfied man—I will
show you a failure.

*Genius is 1 per cent inspiration and 99 per cent perspira-
tion.*

The best thinking has been done in solitude. The worst
has been done in turmoil.

Abraham Lincoln Said

SELECTED BY
RALPH G. NEWMAN

BOOKSELLER AND CIVIL WAR HISTORIAN

EDITOR'S NOTE: *Abraham Lincoln has always been close to the American people, but never more so than now when the nation is facing new crises and also recalling those of a century ago. The following "Words to Live By" were chosen for Lincoln's birthday by Ralph G. Newman, noted authority on Lincolniana. Taken from many places, they combine to make a complete and wonderful expression of a philosophy for free Americans who wish to stay free.*

Honesty. I have always wanted to deal with everyone I meet candidly and honestly. If I have made any assertion not warranted by facts, and it is pointed out to me, I will withdraw it cheerfully.

●

Sincerity. I can only say that I have acted upon my best convictions, without selfishness or malice, and that by the help of God I shall continue to do so.

•

Motives. Ready are we all to cry out and ascribe motives when our toes are pinched.

•

Good and evil. Stand with anybody that stands right. Stand with him while he is right, and part with him when he goes wrong.

•

Law. Let every man remember that to violate the law is to trample on the blood of his father, and to tear that charter of his own and his children's liberty.

•

Success. We can succeed only by concert. It is not "can any of us imagine better?" but, "can we all do better?"

•

Accomplishment. He who does something at the head of one regiment will eclipse him who does nothing at the head of a hundred.

•

Patriotism. Gold is good in its place but living, brave, patriotic men are better than gold.

●

Freedom. As our case is new, so we must think anew, and act anew. We must disenthrall ourselves, and then we shall save our country.

●

America. Fellow citizens, we cannot escape history. We . . . will be remembered in spite of ourselves. No personal significance or insignificance can spare one or another of us. The fiery trial through which we pass will light us down, in honor or dishonor, to the latest generation.

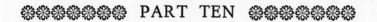

PART TEN

Talismans

*"I believe it would be difficult to find an adult human
being who hasn't a saying or two, or more, that he is
saving because it expresses something vital."*
—DAVID GRAYSON *(See page 13)*

THE INSCRIPTION by Jessica Tandy
LOOK TO THIS DAY by Edward Streeter
MY MAGIC BOOKMARK by Alicia Markova
FAITH—AND FEAR by Ralph Beebe
CAREVILLE, U.S.A. by Conway Fleming Weary

The Inscription

BY

JESSICA TANDY

ACTRESS

> *"Young actors, fear your admirers! Learn in time, from your first steps, to hear, understand and love the cruel truth about yourselves. Find out who can tell you that truth and talk of your art only with those who can tell you the truth."*
>
> —STANISLAVSKY

IT HAPPENED some years ago, at the time when I began acting on the London stage. I had planned to meet an actress friend for an afternoon shopping tour and we had agreed to meet in front of Foyle's famous bookstore in Charing Cross Road.

I arrived a few minutes ahead of time, and rather than

wait for my friend in the damp air of London, I went into Foyle's. Standing near a window where I would be sure to see her coming by, I began to browse among the many books at hand.

The first one I picked up was a collection of 19th century British plays. Nothing extraordinary. But I was stopped by an inscription on the inside cover. I must have read it over four or more times before I could make good sense of the rather strange handwriting. The message printed above was so strong and pertinent for me that I bought the book. After a little research, I discovered that these were the words that had originally been written by the theatrical genius, Stanislavsky.

Later, I placed his quotation on the front page of my first book of press clippings and critical reviews. Throughout my career the thought has served as a guide, for it is wise advice and the kind that can help everyone. Understandably, every human endeavor seeks some expression of approval. But in our eagerness to please and to be pleased with ourselves we choose too often to hear the applause rather than the suggestions for further improvement of our work or ourselves.

It is only when we seek out persons of greater experience than our own and invite their opinions on our projects that we arrive at greater personal development.

All this that I have learned was begun by reading an unknown handwriting in a book at Foyle's in Charing Cross Road.

Look to This Day

BY

EDWARD STREETER

FORMER BANKER,
AUTHOR OF "DERE MABLE,"
"FATHER OF THE BRIDE"
AND "CHAIRMAN OF THE BORED"

> *"Look to this day,*
> *For it is life, the very life of life.*
> *In its brief course lie all the*
> *verities and realities of your existence."*
>
> —UNKNOWN

DURING the first years of depression in the 1930s, a large majority of people of the United States passed almost overnight from a brilliant sunshine to gray gloom. The shock of the transition caused most of us to spend a good part of our time regretting the past and dreading the future.

One day, during this far from gay period, I received from an elderly cousin a card on which was printed a poem. It

179

so happens that some of my best friends are *not* people who send me poems or clippings. Here was an item that was not even accompanied by the note of apology which poem-senders usually enclose.

There it was. Take it or leave it. I almost left it. Then my feeling that relatives were thicker than water caused me to sit down and read it.

What was the poem? It was the one which appears on page 149 in this anthology. A portion of it is also printed above. I read it a second time and then a third. I had it framed and hung it by my bed, a practice to which I am not usually addicted.

Almost a decade later I discovered, in an Adirondack camp, a thin little volume containing an address by the famous physician, Dr. William Osler. It was based on what I had begun to call "my poem," and it stressed the importance of living in what Dr. Osler called "day-tight compartments."

When my friends buttonhole me, however, and tell me of the horrors which they are convinced the future holds in store, or when, with tears in their eyes, they describe the remarkable things that would have happened if they hadn't done what they did do—then I think of this poem.

And I think of something else. I think of the fact that, no matter how brave and strong we may appear, we all need something similar to this poem to which we can cling. Call it what you will—talisman, guidepost, "words to live by." Man has needed them since his cave days and will continue to need them in the eons which lie ahead.

My Magic Bookmark

BY

ALICIA MARKOVA

FAMOUS DANCER

> *"Let nothing disturb thee;*
> *Let nothing dismay thee:*
> *All things pass;*
> *God never changes.*
>
> *Patience attains*
> *All that it strives for.*
> *He who has God*
> *Finds he lacks nothing:*
> *God alone suffices."*
>
> —ST. TERESA OF AVILA

ST. TERESA'S BOOKMARK travels with me everywhere. In a picture frame, it has journeyed around the world with me. Wherever I am, I take it out and set it on my dressing table. And whenever things seem to be going badly, I find comfort in it.

The Bookmark was sent to me when my world seemed to be falling apart. In 1943 I was struck with illness so severe that for the first time in all my long career I was unable to dance. It was frightening. Strength is essential to a ballerina not only in moments of flashing leaps and turns but also for the quiet, controlled movements that give the illusion of being light as thistledown.

I thought—and my thoughts were charged with terror —that I would never again be able to perform in the great and difficult classical ballets to which I had devoted my life.

Then the Bookmark arrived. I read it again and again. Every line offered solace but for me that one line "All things pass" gave me the most comfort and hope. It gave me the patience essential to my recovery. Slowly, I began to realize that pain would pass, and healing come.

Finally, I knew that the message of the Bookmark spoke to me of things other than illness. It spoke to me of a new attitude of mind, an attitude by no means negative. For with patience and fortitude, trouble would pass, releasing energy for positive thought and action.

The months dragged by and at last I was fully recovered. Once more—after a cautious start—I could dance the most exacting roles. And the pain, the heartbreak, the desperation had gone, too, for "All things pass." I was home again; I was living again; I had been reborn.

182

Faith——and Fear

BY

RALPH BEEBE

BOOK PUBLISHER

> *"Fear knocked at the door.*
> *Faith answered.*
> *No one was there."*
>
> —UNKNOWN

EDITOR'S NOTE: *Where did the quotation come from? Here is such information as Mr. Beebe was able to obtain from the present manageress of the Hind's Head Hotel: "The inscription over our fireplace was put up at the time of Dunkirk. I have made many inquiries to try and find out its origin and have been given various answers, but no one has given me chapter and verse. The last information I got about it was in 1959 when a gentleman in London said that it was the Chinese philosopher, Lao-tse, but we have never got down to the real origin of it."*

I READ THESE WORDS over the fireplace of the Hind's Head Hotel in Bray-on-Thames, not far from London, a year

183

ago. They were ascribed to no author, and I had never met them before, but they have been with me since.

Too often fear rules over our lives, intruding into every situation. Fear would sit by our sides and whisper gratuitous advice while we make decisions. Fear would embrace us when we meet grief. Fear would seize our sleeves when we step forward. Fear would fray our bodies and our minds, and rob us of the very sleep we need to mend them.

Fear masquerades in countless forms and under many names: Doubt, Indecision, Procrastination, Alarm, Timidity, Anxiety. In dress clothes, Fear becomes Terror, Horror, Shock, Consternation.

Fear constantly knocks at our door, asking to enter our lives. Fear poses as a friend. Fear claims to be Prudence, Caution, Care, Diligence, and Discretion. But if we open the house of our lives to Fear, we admit a guest who will not soon or gracefully depart.

Faith is the comrade who will serve us best against Fear. For Fear is shadow, but Faith is real. Faith too assumes other shapes and names. There is the Faith that is met as Prayer, the alliance with the Almighty that enables one to meet the contrary ways of the world. Faith is the Courage that has battled for man's highest ideas. Some have known Faith as Will-to-Live when Fear would bring Death also over the threshold. Faith supports us as Confidence, in ourselves and in those we serve and those who serve us.

Keep Faith as a constant companion. When Fear knocks at your door, send Faith to answer. For Faith carries the Light of Truth, dissolving the shadow of Fear that would blot every thought and action.

Careville, U.S.A.

BY

CONWAY FLEMING WEARY

A "THIS WEEK" READER

EDITOR'S NOTE: *Mrs. Conway Fleming Weary is a* This Week *reader who lives in Virginia Beach, Virginia. It was while returning from her husband's class reunion at Williams College not long ago that she saw the sign that became her talisman.*

AS WE WERE driving back from New England to Virginia, somewhere we saw a small sign with an arrow pointing to "Careville." It may have been just an unmapped hamlet, or a name for a rural estate, but many things crowded into my mind at sight of that sign. And it has stayed in my mind ever since.

If only we could *all* move to Careville; not physically, of course, but mentally and spiritually.

Care enough to feel and express our righteous indignation

186

—feel a sense of obligation to sacrifice our personal gain and selfish pursuits for the creation of an America such as we have always dreamed it should be.

Care enough to vote for public servants because they are fine and honest and not because they might benefit us personally in some way.

Care enough to be interested keenly in and to vote for every facet of government in which we truly believe.

Care enough to become fired with a patriotic zeal and purpose that would astound the world and inflame our hearts and minds.

Care for America.

Let's *all* move to Careville!

187

 PART ELEVEN

Legacies

"No man stands alone. Through all the centuries of recorded time, men have set into motion influences that affect your life today."

—WILFERD A. PETERSON

THE TRUMPETER by Christine Hotchkiss

"I DO HEREBY BEQUEATH . . ." by Maude Parker

LETTER TO A LITTLE GIRL by F. Scott Fitzgerald

A THANKSGIVING PRAYER by Louis Bromfield

THE ULTIMATE VICTORY by Dr. Thomas A. Dooley

The Trumpeter

BY

CHRISTINE HOTCHKISS

EDITOR AND AUTHOR
OF "HOME TO POLAND"

"Live as if you were eternal."

—ANDRÉ MAUROIS

RECENTLY, after 18 years, I revisited my Polish homeland. Much had changed, but I found some things still the same.

For example, at Cracow, the ancient capital of Poland, in the very center of town rise the two Gothic towers of the Church of Our Lady Mary. The higher of the two is known as the Tower of the Cracow Trumpeter. From a window far up in the tower, overlooking the market square, at the beginning of each hour of the day, a trumpeter plays a curious little tune called "The Heynal." The distinctive feature of the air is that it breaks off in the middle of a

191

note, as if someone at that moment had snatched the trumpet from his lips. Here is the story:

The notes heard in Cracow today were first sounded over 700 years ago. In the year 1241, a boy trumpeter climbed the tower to sound the alarm as Tartars attacked the city. Seen from the distance by the approaching hordes, he was the target for a shower of arrows. He was near the end of his call when one pierced his throat. That is why the last note begins strongly, trembles and then ceases—broken like the young life of the trumpeter.

The custom has lasted down the centuries. Even during the German occupation and the Russian oppression, the trumpet sounded every hour of the day and night. Today two men from the city's fire brigade are assigned to sound the trumpet's call.

To the Poles, that sharp, clear summons, echoing down through the centuries, is a link with the past and a signal of hope for the future. But more than that, it is a reminder to everybody everywhere that people count—and that if any one of us brings beauty, courage or goodness to the earth, it lives on, as an everlasting legacy of courage and inspiration to those who come after us.

"I Do Hereby Bequeath . . ."

BY

MAUDE PARKER

NOVELIST AND SHORT STORY WRITER

EDITOR'S NOTE: *Maude Parker was for 30 years one of America's best-known woman writers. In addition to many short stories and articles in leading magazines, she wrote ten novels, winning the Mary Roberts Rinehart Prize in 1951 for "Which Mrs. Torr?" One of the few literary forms she was not known to practice was poetry. But after her death in 1959 her husband, Edmund W. Pavenstedt, found among her papers the poem below, written for her two grown daughters. He showed it to a friend, a well-known poet, who called it "a remarkable testament of a remarkable mind and soul." Mr. Pavenstedt had the poem privately printed and bound for Maude Parker's many friends. It is printed here with his special permission.*

> *This is my legacy—*
> Not property real and tangible
> Nor stocks and bonds which could be sold—

But these few words, garnered from years
Numbering half a hundred.

I do hereby bequeath, give, pass title unto
This extract of experience
To my beloved daughters,
Share and share alike:

Nothing that lives, stands still.
Grow it must, or shrink;
There is no alternative.
Only inanimate things are static, fixed.
Marble remains unchanged;
The living creature changes always:
Expands, increases—or retrogrades,
Withers to decay.

Stretch your mind,
Even as you stretch your arms
Upward to the sky
Lest numbness should set in.
So stretch your mind,
Give it a daily task beyond its present strength;
And store it each day with treasure:
Poetry to say under your breath,
Knowledge newly acquired.

Judge yourself more strictly
Than you judge your neighbors,
Yet weigh no human on a scales

Designed for saints;
Be almost as forgiving to yourself
As you would be to strangers:
If it were arrogance to ask perfection
Uniquely from yourself.
(If you desire humility, regard
The earth itself, the sky
In all its changing aspects—
Sun, rain, and mist,
Lightning and moonlight.)

Give without stint—
I need not tell you this—
But teach yourself also to accept
What others give. Not heedlessly,
Nor with false pride. Not
As your just due,
Your merited deserving,
Nor as an almoner.
Rather, in recognition
Of another's overflowing heart.

And stretch your soul:
Beyond the confines of forgiveness, understanding.
Know this: Inscribe it as a truth:
The irreparable loss is to the betrayer,
Never to the betrayed;
The one who deals the mortal blow
Receives the mortal wound.

Letter to a Little Girl

BY

F. SCOTT FITZGERALD

EDITOR'S NOTE: *For all of his preoccupation with the jazz age in which he lived, F. Scott Fitzgerald was a devoted father. His daughter—and only child—Frances was one of his main concerns throughout his otherwise unconventional life. She is now the wife of a Washington lawyer and mother of four children. In 1933, when she was 11 years old, and away at camp, Fitzgerald wrote a letter to her which ended with the following wonderful, whimsical advice.*

The letter (copyright 1945 by New Directions) is reprinted in a new book of letters, The Father, *Evan Jones, editor, published in March 1960 by Rinehart and Company. Dated 1933, this Fitzgerald father-daughter advice is delightful reading any time, but especially on Father's Day!*

DEAR PIE:

- *Things to worry about:*

  Worry about courage
  Worry about cleanliness

196

Worry about efficiency

Worry about horsemanship. . . .

- *Things not to worry about:*

    Don't worry about popular opinion

    Don't worry about dolls

    Don't worry about the past

    Don't worry about the future

    Don't worry about growing up

    Don't worry about anybody getting ahead of you

    Don't worry about triumph

    Don't worry about failure unless it comes through
          your own fault

    Don't worry about mosquitoes

    Don't worry about flies

    Don't worry about insects in general

    Don't worry about parents

    Don't worry about boys

    Don't worry about disappointments

    Don't worry about pleasures

    Don't worry about satisfactions

- *Things to think about:*

    What am I really aiming at?

                                        SCOTT

197

A Thanksgiving Prayer

BY

LOUIS BROMFIELD

FAMOUS AMERICAN NOVELIST

Oh Lord, I thank you for the privilege and gift of living in a world filled with beauty and excitement and variety.

I thank you for the gift of loving and being loved, for the friendliness and understanding and beauty of the animals on the farm and in the forest and marshes, for the green of the trees, the sound of a waterfall, the darting beauty of the trout in the brook.

I thank you for the delights of music and children, of other men's thoughts and conversation and their books to read by the fireside or in bed with the rain falling on the roof or the snow blowing past outside the window.

I thank you for the beauties of the four seasons and of the churches and the houses built by fellow men that stand throughout the centuries as monuments to man's aspirations and sense of beauty.

I thank you for the powers of mind which find in the universe an endless and inexhaustible source of interest and fascination, for the understanding of so many elements which make life precious.

I thank you for all the senses you have bestowed upon me and for the delights which they bring me. I thank you for my body itself which is so wonderful and delightful a mechanism.

I thank you for the smile on the face of a woman, for the touch of a friend's hand, for the laughter of a child, the wagging tail of a dog and the touch of his cold nose against my face.

I thank you for all of these things and many more, and above all I thank you for people with all their goodness and understanding which so far outweigh their vices, their envy, their deceits.

Thank you, God, for life itself, without which the universe would have no meaning.

The Ultimate Victory

BY

DR. THOMAS A. DOOLEY

EDITOR'S NOTE: *The late Dr. Dooley, known to thousands of his native patients in Laos as "Dr. Tom," was a great medical missionary, builder of hospitals, humanitarian. He was also a man of profound religious faith. One of his last letters, written from a hospital in Hong Kong to Father Theodore Hesburgh, president of Notre Dame University, contains this unforgettable passage:*

WHEN THE TIME COMES, like now, then the storm around me does not matter. Nothing human or earthly can touch me. A wilder storm of peace gathers in my heart. What seems unpossessable, I can possess. . . . What is un-utterable, I can utter. Because I can pray, I can communicate. How do people endure anything on earth if they can-not have God?

PART TWELVE

For a Better America

"We here in America, hold in our hands the hope of the world, the fate of the coming years; and shame and disgrace will be ours if in our eyes the light of high resolve is dimmed, if we trail in the dust the golden hopes of men."

—THEODORE ROOSEVELT

THE TIME IS NOW by Charles H. Malik

THE BEST-KEPT SECRET by John W. Gardner

THE STRENUOUS LIFE by Bruce Catton

TWO KINDS OF PEOPLE by Roger Hull

HOW TO BUILD A BETTER TOMORROW
by Herbert Hoover

ON BEING AMERICAN by George D. Mardikian

THE SPARK WITHIN by William Nichols

The Time Is Now

BY

CHARLES H. MALIK

FORMER PRESIDENT,
UNITED NATIONS GENERAL ASSEMBLY

"The fault, dear Brutus, is not in our stars,
But in ourselves, that we are underlings."

—WILLIAM SHAKESPEARE

WE—ALL OF US—need a mighty spiritual revival. The ideal of a settled, successful, selfish life is wholly inadequate. One craves to see great themes sought and discussed, great causes espoused. One burns for the reintroduction into life of the pursuit of greatness. Everywhere I go I find people sitting on the edge of their seats waiting to be shown the way.

There are infinite possibilities, both material and moral, to vindicate freedom against unfreedom, joy of living against tyranny, man against all that is subhuman and inhuman, truth against darkness and falsehood, and God against the devil and his works. The time is here now, today—a time not for pessimism and despair, but for a vast advance on many fronts.

The Best-Kept Secret

BY

JOHN W. GARDNER

PRESIDENT OF THE
CARNEGIE CORPORATION

*"We must produce a great age, or see the collapse of
the upward striving of our race."*

—ALFRED NORTH WHITEHEAD

THE BEST-KEPT secret in America today is that people
would rather work hard for something they believe in than
enjoy a pampered idleness. They would rather sacrifice their
comfort for an honored objective than bask in extravagant
leisure.

Every man knows that there is exhilaration in intense
effort applied toward a meaningful end. Ask the physician
at the height of his powers whether he would trade his life,
with its 18-hour days, its midnight calls, its pressures and

anxieties, for a life of idleness in tranquil surroundings. Ask the retired businessman whether he would trade his leisure for a job in which he could apply his full powers toward something he believed in.

Since the beginning of time, most humans have had to work hard either because physical survival demanded it or because their taskmasters required it. Today, thanks to prosperity, we don't have to put out great effort for physical survival; and a free people has no taskmasters. There is no one to tell us what to do. And so *we must decide for ourselves*. What we have to learn is that free men must seek and set their own goals.

The Strenuous Life

BY

BRUCE CATTON

PULITZER PRIZE HISTORIAN
AND AUTHOR OF ''THE COMING FURY''

"Let us live in the harness, striving mightily."

—THEODORE ROOSEVELT

THEODORE ROOSEVELT preached the strenuous life—
and practiced what he preached. Whether he was sparring
with a professional boxer, hiking in Washington's Rock
Creek Park or taking time off from a busy life to hunt big
game, he kept eternally active. And he thought everybody
else ought to do the same.

Since he left the White House, modern life has become
pretty well padded, and most of us like it that way. Why
walk half a mile when you can get in the car and drive?

Why exert muscles when so many muscle-saving devices are available? Wasn't T.R. just a little bit hipped on the subject?

Maybe so. But Roosevelt was not just talking about physical exercise for its own sake. He was discussing the basic terms on which human life has to be lived—and with special reference to his own country. What he said is still worth listening to.

"I preach to you, then, my countrymen," he once said, "that our country calls not for the life of ease, but the life of strenuous endeavor. The twentieth century looms before us big with the fate of many nations.

"If we stand idly by . . . if we shrink from the hard contests where men must win at hazard of their lives and at the risk of all they hold dear, then the bolder and stronger peoples will pass us by, and will win for themselves the domination of the world."

Whether we like it or not, that makes sense. America is a demanding country. Simply because it offers us more than any other country offers its people, it expects more in return. And the twentieth century, for all that it is studded with gadgets and luxuries, is still lived on primitive terms. It is not likely to change in the visible future.

Two Kinds of People

BY

ROGER HULL

BUSINESS EXECUTIVE

*"If everyone swept his own doorstep, then the whole
wide world would be clean."*

—PROVERB

HAVE YOU ever asked yourself this question: If every
citizen performed just as you do, where would the country
be? What if every fellow worked at his job the way you
work, showed the same interest, the same diligence, the
same faithfulness, the same skill and discipline? What would
happen to our country?

Someone has aptly said that there are really only two
kinds of people: those who are part of the problem and
those who are part of the solution.

Well, what about you?

Do you think only in terms of yourself—how much you can make, what you can get out of life? Those who think that way are definitely part of the problem.

Or are you concerned with the contribution you can make —how much you can give, how much you can put in? People like that are part of the answer.

Some people treat life like a slot machine, trying to put in as little as possible, and always hoping to hit the jackpot. But I believe that people are wiser, happier, and have more inner peace when they think of life as a solid, intelligent investment from which they receive in terms of what they put in. And by so doing they help preserve our free society.

How to Build
a Better Tomorrow

BY

HERBERT HOOVER

FORMER PRESIDENT
OF THE UNITED STATES

"Those who cannot remember the past are condemned to repeat it."

—GEORGE SANTAYANA

PEOPLE OFTEN wonder why historians go to so much trouble to preserve millions of books, documents and records of the past. Why do we have libraries? What good are these documents and the history books? Why do we record and save the actions of men, the negotiations of statesmen and the campaigns of armies?

Because, sometimes, the voice of experience can cause us

to stop, look, and listen. And because, sometimes, past records, correctly interpreted, can give us warning of what to do and what not to do.

If we are ever to create enduring peace, we must seek its origins in human experience and in the record of human idealism. From the story of the fortitude, courage, and devotion of men and women, we create the inspirations of youth. From stories of the Christian saints, right down to Budapest's heroic martyrs, history records the suffering, the self-denial, the devotion and the heroic deeds of men. Surely from these records there can come help to mankind in our confusions and perplexities, and in our yearnings for peace.

The supreme purpose of history is a better world. History gives a warning to those who would promote war. History brings inspiration to those who seek peace. In short, history helps us learn. Yesterday's records can keep us from repeating yesterday's mistakes. And from the pieces of mosaic assembled by historians comes wisdom to guide the progress of America and the progress of mankind.

On Being American

BY

GEORGE D. MARDIKIAN

ARMENIAN-BECOME-AMERICAN,
AUTHOR OF "SONG OF AMERICA"

"——to every man his chance
——to every man, regardless of his birth,
his shining, golden opportunity
——to every man the right to live, to work,
to be himself, and to become whatever his
manhood and his vision can combine to make
him
——this, seeker, is the promise of America."

—THOMAS WOLFE

THE OTHER DAY, in Seattle, Washington, I gave a talk before several hundred people, and told them that I thought America was a strong, beautiful, and righteous country. A young man came up to me afterward and said with a knowing smile, "No wonder you go about singing the praise of

213

America. In Europe, you were nothing. America has made you rich and famous." Before I could reply he was gone.

It's true America has been good to me, and I count my blessings every day. But I wanted to find that young man and say, "You miss my point. The priceless thing America has given to me has nothing to do with money or fame. Some would call it national pride. I call it the dignity of being American."

To someone born here—born free—it's hard to understand. He's never known what it is to be without it. I was born in Armenia. Today, I cannot find my Armenia—the Armenia of my fathers—on the map.

Forty years ago, when I came to America, I had to flee my home like a criminal. Yet my only crime was being an Armenian. That July morning, when I first saw the Statue of Liberty from the deck of the immigrant steamer, it was like suddenly hearing a hymn of hope. I lifted my head, and my heart. I took deep breaths of the fresh harbor air. For the first time in my life, I felt free—thrillingly and blessedly free.

This, thank God, is not a private experience. There are millions like me in America today—fugitives from unhappy lands across the seas. We're grateful of course for our three meals a day, and our jobs, and for the opportunities that America has so generously given to us and our children.

But we'd fight and die before we'd give up that feeling of dignity—that right to hold up our heads, look the world in the eye, and call ourselves Americans.

The Spark Within

BY

WILLIAM NICHOLS

EDITOR OF "THIS WEEK" MAGAZINE

"The stop-watch of history is running. The race is on . . ."

—DWIGHT D. EISENHOWER

SOMETHING IMPORTANT is happening in America to-day: changing conditions in the world are stripping away a great illusion which, more than anything, has contributed to our sense of moral slackness and discontent.

This illusion was the belief that America, following our victory in World War II, was entitled to easy, automatic, prosperous, and perpetual leadership throughout the free world.

But now, with the emergence of many new nations and groups of nations, we find that this assumption is being challenged on every front—political, economic, military, and cultural. In short, a new balance of power is forming, and it is forcing us to reappraise and reassert ourselves as a nation.

Suddenly we are aroused from our easy affluence to find that this is no longer a one-power world, where we rule the roost; nor a two-power world, where we can comfortably blame all our troubles on a single wicked foe. No, now it has become a multipower world, filled with new groupings of races and nations, all of them fiercely competitive, and many of them actively hostile to the United States.

What I predict, as a result of these realignments, is the emergence of a new nationalism and a new morality which will shatter all sense of complacency from stem to stern. As these trends develop, they are bound, I believe, to affect the thinking of all our people—and to affect it for the better.

This new nationalism is not to be confused with "Fourth of July patriotism." It is certainly not the boastful chauvinism so often charged to Americans. Patriotism is a fine and positive force if it inspires us to win by being better; it can be negative, vicious, and destructive if it makes us smug, lazy, arrogant, or complacent.

The new nationalism must be something more than patriotism. It rests on our awakening to the hard facts of life —facts measured in such terms as gold movements, balance of trade, world prices, atomic inventions and votes in the United Nations. Against this background, the central themes are competence and competition—good, heads-up, old-fashioned competition, where the rewards and recognitions are based on excellence, effort, ability, and inner discipline. It requires the creative best of every individual if we are to reassert our claim to leading the world.

For leadership is not a perpetual right. Leadership must be earned and re-earned, day after day. This is America's challenge—and *the race is on!*

My Own Words to Live By

BY

THE READER

Index of Quotations

❋

221

Index of Contributors